An Illustrated
History of Music
for Young Musicians

THE CLASSICAL PERIOD

Gilles Comeau
Rosemary Covert

Thanks

The authors and publisher wish to thank the persons in charge of librairies, museums, galleries, and private collections, named below, for permitting the reproduction of works of art in their collection.

Albright-Knox Gallery, Buffalo; Alinari/Scala/Art Ressource; Alison Frantz, Princeton; Archiv für Kunst und Geschichte, Berlin; Archives Mondadori; Archives Skira; Art Institute of Chicago; Ashmolean Museum, Oxford; Bergane, Academia Carrara; Bernand; Bettmann Archive; Bevolina; Bibliothèque de l'opéra, Paris; Bibliothèque de Versailles; Bibliothèque du Conservatoire; Bibliothèque nationale, Paris; Bildarchiv Foto Marburg; Bildarchiv Preussischer Kulturbesitz, Berlin; Boymans-Van Beuningen Museum, Rotterdam; Bridgeman Art Gallery/Thomas Cordham Foundation; Bridgeman Art Library; British Library, London; Carl Wilhelm Holdermann/Weimar, Staatsliche Kunstsammlungen, Schlossmuseum; Château de Versailles; Civico Museo Bibliografico Musicale, Bologne; Clive Barda; Cornaro Chapel, Santa Maria della Vittoria, Rome; Detroit Institute of Arts; Deutsche Staatsbibliotek; Galleria Borghese, Rome; Germanisches Nationalmuseum, Nürnburg; Gesellschaft der Musikfreunde, Vienna; Giraudeau Bridgeman; Giraudon, Paris; Heimatmuseum, Cothën; Hulton-Deutsch Collection; Johnny Van Heften Gallery, London; Kunsthistorishe Museum, Vienna; Kunstsammlungen zu Weimar; Kupferstichkabinett, Dresden; Ludovico Canelli, Rome; Mander and Mitchenson Theatre Collection; Mansell Collection; Metropolitan Museum of Art, The Crosby Brown Collection of Musical Instruments; Musée Barbier-Muller, Geneva; Musée de Cambrai, Cambrai; Musée de Versailles; Musées nationales, Paris; Musée du Louvre, Paris; Museo Civico d'Arte Antico, Turin; Museo Correr, Venice; Museo del Prado, Madrid; Museum of Modern Art, New York; National Gallery of Art, Washington; National Gallery, London; National Monuments Record Centre, Royal Commission on the Historical Monuments of England; National Portrait Gallery, London; Nymphenburg Gardens, Munich; Peter Newark's Pictures; Picturepoint/Civico Museo Bibliografica Musicale, Bologna; Prussian State Library, Berlin; R. M. N., Paris; Real Biblioteca de San Lorenzo de el Escorial, Madrid; Rijksmuseum, Amsterdam; Royal Collection, Hampton Court Palace, Her Majesty the Queen; Sotheby's, London; SPADEM, R.M.N.; Staatliche Kunstsammlungen, Dresden; Staats-und Universitatsbibliotek, Hamburg; Stadzarchiv, Arnstadt; Szépmüversity Museum, Budapest; Tate Gallery, London; The Hulton-Deutsch Collection; The Playing Card Museum, U.S. Playing Card Co., Cincinnati; The Royal Collection, London; Ullstein; VEB Deutscher Verlag Für Musik Leipzig/Werner Reinhold; Victoria and Albert Museum, London; Wallraf-Richartz-Museum, Cologna; Yale Centre for British Art;

Cover & design   : Martine Mongrain and Marie-Josée Hotte
Printer   : Centre franco-ontarien de ressources pédagogiques

© CFORP, 1998
   290 Dupuis Street, Vanier, Ontario K1L 1A2
      Phone orders: (613) 747-1553
         Fax: (613) 747-0866
      Web site: http://www.cforp.on.ca
         E-mail: cforp@cforp.on.ca

ISBN 2-89442-758-1
Copyright — fourth semester 1998
National Library of Canada
                    Printed in Canada

PREFACE

For many decades now, programmes of European concert music have largely been drawn from the period we call the Classical, from approximately 1750 to 1825. Even so, performers and writers about this music have not understood its roots. Instead, the music of this period has been viewed from musical values and ideals that were formulated in the succeeding era known as the Romantic. The publication of Charles Rosen's landmark work on the Classical period corrected this misguided view but even so, our ideas about the music from this period have been slow to change.

I am delighted that this attractive introduction to the Classical period of European concert music is now available. It shows how the music was closely tied to developments in life style and politics in Europe and North America. The rallying cry for this period, Jean-Jacques Rousseau's "Back to nature," was based on communal values, not the viewpoint of one individual as was the case in the later Romantic period. Perhaps it was this emphasis on community that encouraged the development of chamber music works like duo sonatas, trios, and string quartets during this period. The symphony, too, as it developed during the Classical period, was based on the pattern of conversation between individuals and groups. Differences of sound quality and strength were celebrated, but each voice remained an important part of the whole. Probably the most important change from the previous Baroque period was that voices making up the texture of a work frequently changed their level of prominence. No longer was the low bass line ruling over all of the other voices in the texture!

With this guide in hand, I hope that you and your child will enjoy discovering, listening to, and performing the wonderful repertoire of the Classical period.

Dr. Elaine Keillor
Professor
Carleton University

Table of Contents

Introduction

The History of Music 7

The Classical Period 7

The Classical Era

Life in the Classical Era 8

    The Political Situation 8

    Society and Customs 16

    Science and Thought 22

Art in the Classical Era 25

    The Early Period 25

    The Late Period 28

Musical Life in the Classical Era 32

    The Patronage System in Transition 32

Music in the Classical Period

Characteristics of Music in the Classical Period 35

    General Features 35

    Specific Features 36

    Musical Forms 39

    Vocal Music 42

    Instrumental Music 45

Composers of the Classical Period

Lesser Known Classical Composers 52

Joseph Haydn (1732–1809) 56

    Early Years 56

    Career 57

    Music 62

Wolfgang Amadeus Mozart (1756-1791) 65

    Early Years 65

    Early Career 70

    Personal Life 71

    Later Career 72

    The Last Year 75

    Music 76

Ludwig van Beethoven (1770-1827) 80

    Early Years 80

    Early Career 82

    Personal Life 84

    Later Career 86

    Music 87

The History of Music

Over the years, music in the Western world has been changing constantly and the music of today is very different from the music people made 300 years ago.

To help you understand how this music has developed, each of the books in this series will describe a different musical period. For each era, we will show you the way the people of the time lived, and the kinds of art and architecture that were typical of the period. We will discuss the important musical characteristics and describe the lives and contributions of the major composers.

The history of Western music is usually divided into six broad time periods:

Middle Ages	Renaissance	Baroque	Classical	Romantic	Contemporary
	1450	1600	1750	1825	1900

This book presents the Classical period.

The Classical Period

The Classical period is generally taken to begin in 1750 with the death of Johann Sebastian Bach, and end about 75 years later, around 1825, when the Romantic movement was becoming predominant, and close to the year of death (1827) of Ludwig van Beethoven, the last great Classical master. It was a period of transition in which political changes were reflected by changes in the art, architecture and music of the time.

You may find the word "classical" confusing, because we use it in different ways. We talk about classical music, the music written by composers such as Bach, Beethoven and Chopin as opposed to other kinds of music like folk songs, pop music, jazz or the musical traditions of other cultures. We also talk about the Classical period, with the word "classical"capitalized, in the history of Western music. The Classical period was a particular time in Western history when people became fascinated with the ancient civilizations of Greece and Rome. They admired the ideals of moderation, order and simplicity that originated in these ancient societies and tried to return to those ideals. Inspired by the perfect proportions of a Greek temple, artists tried to achieve the same satisfying balance in their own works, whether in architecture, painting or music.

The final years of absolute monarchy in France

In the 1700s, most European states were ruled by kings and queens whose power was limitless and who derived their authority directly from God. Louis XIV of France was the most powerful of them all. His court and his palace at Versailles illustrated all the excesses that were possible in an absolute monarchy. His successors, Louis XV and XVI, continued in his footsteps, and their incompetent leadership was a major cause of the people's revolt that became the French revolution.

Louis XVI of France

His wife, Marie Antoinette

Other European rulers

Other absolute monarchs of the period were Catherine the Great of Russia, Frederick the Great of Prussia, the Empress Maria Theresa of Austria, and her son, Joseph II. Some of them, like Frederick the Great and Joseph II, were more in tune with the desire for reform and introduced change without revolution.

Catherine the Great of Russia, her husband Peter III and their son Paul. Peter III was not popular with his subjects. They overthrew him and put Catherine on the throne instead.

Frederick the Great of Prussia

Empress Maria Theresa of Austria

Joseph II of Austria

The seeds of revolution

Voltaire, J.-A. Houdon, 1781.

Houdon, the famous French sculptor, captures the glint in Voltaire's eye, as though the philosopher was about to deliver one of his famous bons mots.

The Enlightenment was a philosophical movement that originated primarily in France, led by philosopher-writers like Voltaire and Jean-Jacques Rousseau. Adherents to the movement believed in the power of human reason. They thought that if men could discover the underlying laws of nature, as Isaac Newton had explained the laws of gravity, they could also understand the laws governing society and human behaviour. With understanding could come change.

The philosophers of the Enlightenment wanted to build systems of government that were free from the tyranny that could exist in an absolute monarchy. In this they were influenced by the English philosopher John Locke, who held that all people were born good, independent and equal. He believed that governments derived their right to govern from the consent of the people, not from any hereditary rights granted by God.

John Locke attacked the theory of the divine right of kings which gave monarchies the authority to hold power.

Jean-Jacques Rousseau believed that man in his natural state was inherently virtuous and therefore superior to civilized man. That is why this engraving shows him in a natural setting, which was unusual for portraits at the time.

The American Revolution (1775–1783)

It was under the influence of Enlightenment ideas that the American Revolution was born. The original 13 colonies established in North America were under the control of Britain. As they became richer and more solidly established, the colonists began to resent the rule of the British monarchy and to think that they had the right to decide their own destiny. With the Declaration of Independence in 1776, the American colonists announced their independence. The British government retaliated by sending in the army, but the war that resulted was won by the Americans. Their victory created a new country, the United States of America, a republic governed by the people's elected officials. The new country was based on the idea that "all men are created equal, that they are endowed by their Creator with certain inalienable Rights, that among these are Life, Liberty, and the pursuit of Happiness." These rights guaranteed the citizens freedom of thought, freedom of the press, freedom of religion and the right to trial by jury, protecting them from the arbitrary rule of any monarch.

The first American flag, with 13 stars and 13 stripes representing the original 13 colonies.

Thomas Jefferson, by Houdon. Jefferson was the architect of the Declaration of Independence.

The Declaration of Independence was signed on July 4, 1776.

The document proclaimed the natural rights of man in an age of absolute monarchy. It had a tremendous impact in America and in Europe.

The French Revolution (1789–1799)

The *Déclaration des droits de l'homme et du citoyen* [The declaration of the rights of men and citizens] was directly inspired by the American Declaration of Independence and Bill of Rights, and the ideas of the Enlightenment. It declared the natural right of man to freedom, equality, property and security, and the right to resist oppression. The new French society was to be built on the will of the people.

The French Revolution was inspired by the ideas of the Enlightenment and the American Declaration of Independence. Opposition to the monarchy spread from the property owners and the middle classes to the peasants, and resulted in a bloody uprising. The motto of the revolutionaries was "Liberty, equality, fraternity." The monarchy was abolished and many aristocrats were put to death by guillotine, including Louis XVI and his queen, Marie Antoinette. During the 10 years of the revolution, there were a series of governments that developed the laws by which the new republic would rule itself. Aristocratic privilege was destroyed, and land was redistributed. Taxes now applied to everyone, not just the middle and lower classes.

Prise des palais des Tuileries, le 10 avril, 1792, Jean Duplessis-Bertaux. Here we see the revolutionaries capturing Marie Antoinette's palace, called the Tuileries, where the king and queen were hiding.

This painting shows the execution of Louis XVI, the reigning monarch in France at the time of the Revolution.

Some famous faces from the French Revolution

Georges Jacques Danton (1759–1794)

Danton was a member of the Committee for Public Safety, the ruling body of the revolutionary government. His inclination to compromise caused him to be accused of being an enemy of the revolution and sent to the guillotine.

Jean-Paul Marat (1743–1793)

Marat was a journalist and the editor of a radical newspaper that advocated violence against the supporters of Louis XVI. He was stabbed to death in his bath by Charlotte Corday, who held him responsible for the Reign of Terror.

Maximilien de Robespierre (1758–1794)

As the most powerful member of the Committee for Public Safety, Robespierre tried to eliminate everyone he considered to be an enemy of the revolution. Thousands were sent to the guillotine in what became known as the Reign of Terror. In the end he was overthrown, and executed.

Rouget de Lisle, the composer, sings the song he called the War Song of the Army of the Rhine, later to become known as the Marseillaise. Sung by revolutionary soldiers from Marseilles as they entered Paris, the song became the national anthem of the new republic and has remained so ever since.

The working-class heroes of the French Revolution were called *sans culottes*, meaning "without breeches," because they wore the trousers typical of the labouring classes.

Napoleon Bonaparte

Emperor Napoleon I,
painted by Ingres

In 1799, dissatisfaction with the ineffectiveness of a series of revolutionary governments reached a peak. A group led by a young general and hero of the French army, Napoleon Bonaparte, seized power by force. They set up a government called the Consulate, with Napoleon as First Consul. Napoleon did many good things. He established the Bank of France, the French education system and the Napoleonic Code, incorporating in law many of the changes introduced during the revolution. But in 1804, he crowned himself Emperor of France, returning the country to the absolute monarchy the people had fought a bloody revolution to remove.

The Coronation of Napoleon and Josephine,
Jacques-Louis David, 1805–1807

The Napoleonic Wars

Napoleon's primary genius was as a military commander. By 1812, France had conquered most of Europe. His downfall was his ambition, which led him to invade Russia. His army was forced into retreat, and was virtually wiped out by the terrible winter conditions. Then the armies of all the countries he had conquered rallied to fight against him, and the leaders of his own army refused to follow his orders. In 1814, he was forced to step down as Emperor, and banished to the Mediterranean island of Elba. All Europe breathed a sigh of relief. A year later, though, he escaped and returned to France. His old soldiers flocked to his side as he marched toward Paris. In the end, however, he was defeated on the fields of Belgium by the British army under the Duke of Wellington. This time he was banished to St. Helena, a distant and more isolated island in the South Atlantic. He died there of stomach cancer in 1821.

Napoleon at Arcole,
Antoine-Jean Gros, 1796

The famous French painter David's conception of Napoleon as hero

The rise of the middle class

Many works by the French painter Chardin illustrate the lives of the poor, like this laundress and her child.

At the beginning of the Classical era, European society was organized the same way it had always been. The privileged ones were the land-owning aristocrats, plus a small middle class, made up of merchants, lawyers, doctors and perhaps bankers. There was a huge gap between their standard of living and that of the people at the other end of the scale, the poor craftspeople, servants and farm labourers.

One major change taking place, however, was the spread of literacy. No longer was the ability to read restricted to the aristocracy and the church. And with the period of revolution, some redistribution of land, power and money did take place, particularly in France but in other countries as well. The nobility still existed, but their circumstances were often reduced. More people moved into the middle class, and they made gains in power and influence. More and more, they were the people who were buying books, paintings, sculptures, going to concerts and hiring people to design and build nice houses for them. For the people at the bottom though, the peasants and domestic servants, life did not get very much easier.

Chardin, *The Scullery Maid*

The scullery maid was employed to wash the dishes and pots and pans. Here you see her scrubbing a long-handled pan used to cook over the open fire in the kitchen.

A picnic for the well-to-do

Living conditions

Although living conditions for the poor were as meagre as ever, the wealthier classes became more comfortable during the years of the Classical period. The growth of the middle class meant that more people were able to afford things that were previously only available to the very rich. With increased trade and communication, elegant styles in furniture and home decoration spread from France, the hub of fashion, to other countries in Europe.

No matter how well off people were, however, they could never have lived with any degree of comfort without servants to do all the heavy work. No one had running water, so someone had to bring the water into the house and carry it into the kitchen for cooking and cleaning, and upstairs to all the bedrooms for washing. An early version of the flush toilet had been invented, but its use was rare. Most people used chamber pots: the servants would dispose of the contents in cesspits. Candles and oil lamps were the only way to light your house and for most of the period, city streets were dark at night.

Travel was still difficult, slow and uncomfortable. Even those who could afford to travel by carriage did not have a very comfortable ride. The lower classes had to travel by foot, so they tended to spend most of their lives without even leaving the place they were born.

Mozart wrote to his father about his trip to Munich in 1780, "Why that carriage jolted the very souls out of our bodies! And the seats! Hard as a rock! After we left Wasserburg I really thought I would never get my behind to Munich in one piece! It became quite sore and no doubt was fiery red. For two whole stages I sat with my hands dug into the upholstery and my behind suspended in the air."

This picture illustrates a well-to-do family enjoying their comfortable living room.

The era of the salon

Madame de Sorquinville,
by Letourneau

This painting of Madame de Sorquinville, a salon hostess, shows her as a woman of intelligence and humour, rather than merely a fashion plate.

The 18th century was a time that valued intellectual achievement. People were sought after for their wit and sensitivity, and elegant conversation was an art to be cultivated. This was the heyday of the salon, a gathering at the home of a fashionable woman that was partly a social event, partly a seminar, where art, music, books and ideas were discussed. The institution was invented in France but spread to other countries as well, and from the aristocracy to the wealthier middle classes. Presiding over a salon was one way for a woman of wit and intelligence to have some influence in a society run by men. She could create a place where people came together to discuss ideas in a way that they could not at a royal court, for instance, for fear of offending the ruler. She could invite the important people she knew and expose them to the ideas of a philosopher, the music of a new composer, a recent book from a well-known writer. Invitations to the most prestigious salons were a mark of social acceptance, and were highly sought after.

First Reading of Voltaire's Orphan of China *at Madame Geoffrin's Salon in 1755, A.C.C. Lemonnier*

The role of women in society

The philosophers and intellectuals of the enlightenment, who wrote so movingly about the rights of man, did not extend these rights to everyone. Excluded were poor people with no land and no education, and women in general. In most European countries, women were considered the property of their fathers until they were handed over to a husband. Since most women were not expected to have a life outside the family, there were very few who became powerful. In the 1700s there were two exceptions to this rule, the Empress Maria Theresa of Austria, and Catherine the Great of Russia. Maria Theresa inherited her throne from her father, but had to go to war to defend her right to it, and Catherine was put on the throne of Russia when her husband offended too many of his influential subjects.

Women did write and paint and compose, but to be recognized outside their own social circle for their talents was quite rare. One of the world's great novelists, Jane Austen, author of *Pride and Prejudice* and *Emma*, did not at first have her name printed on the title pages of her books, although she did achieve wide recognition by the end of her life. Marie Antoinette's favourite painter was a woman, Élisabeth Vigée-Lebrun. Madame Lebrun became well known for her portraits and was even elected to the exclusive French Academy. Only a few women composers managed to have their works published. Women did have a real impact on musical life, however, as teachers, singers, authors of instruction manuals and as patrons and organizers of musical events.

According to Jean-Jacques Rousseau, one of the philosophers of the Enlightenment, "Women in general possess no artistic sensibility. The celestial fire that ignites the soul... the inspiration that consumes... the sublime ecstasies that reside in the depths of the heart are always lacking in women's writings. Their creations are as cold and pretty as women themselves."

Jane Austin was the daughter of a country parson who lived her whole life with her family.

Élisabeth Vigée-Lebrun, *Self-Portrait*

Madame de Pompadour was the powerful mistress of Louis XV of France. She was an important figure both at court and in salon society, and exerted her influence on behalf of several artists and philosophers.

Women's clothing

This stiff-looking dress supported by enormous panniers worn in 1765 by Maria Louisa, the Queen of Spain, was out of style in France by 1750.

Women's clothing changed drastically during the Classical era. At the beginning of the period, styles in France, the world leader in fashion, had moved away from dresses with huge skirts held out by panniers, although dresses in this style were still worn in other countries. The new look was the *robe à la française*. A woman still wore corsets underneath, but the dress looked softer and more natural. It fastened in the front, and opened up to show an underskirt decorated with flounces. The sleeves too ended in lacy flounces, and the neckline was decorated with ribbons and lace.

During the revolution, when excess was frowned upon and naturalness was in vogue, women's fashions became much simpler. After the revolution, there was a radical change in women's clothing towards what was seen as the classical style of ancient Greece. Gone were the silks and brocades, gone were the corsets that had to be laced up tightly. Instead women wore high-waisted, short-sleeved dresses of lightweight fabrics that draped naturally over the body. The most daring women dampened their gauzes with water to make them hug the figure even more.

These two sisters are dressed in the neoclassical style: the dresses are long and slim, and their hairstyles look like the ones seen on the women in Greek and Roman statues.

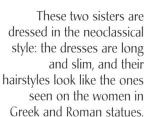

This painting of the Marquise de Pompadour by Boucher shows her wearing a *robe à la française*.

Men's styles

At the beginning of the Classical period, well-to-do men still wore knee breeches and powdered wigs. The wigs gradually became smaller and more natural looking, with a small pigtail in the back, until they were done away with entirely during the revolutionary period. The other major change that came from the revolution was the return of trousers, which had not been worn for the last 600 years. No major change in men's fashion has occurred since.

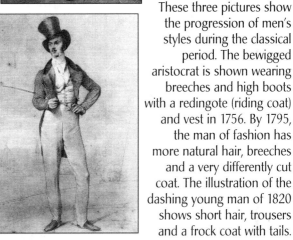

These three pictures show the progression of men's styles during the classical period. The bewigged aristocrat is shown wearing breeches and high boots with a redingote (riding coat) and vest in 1756. By 1795, the man of fashion has more natural hair, breeches and a very differently cut coat. The illustration of the dashing young man of 1820 shows short hair, trousers and a frock coat with tails.

Clothing for the ordinary people

Middle-class people wore much simpler clothing. The painting below by Jean-Baptiste Chardin shows a woman and her daughter, dressed similarly. The mother wears a dress that is tucked up to show her skirt, with a cape and a modest bonnet. The daughter's only touch of elegance is the fur trim on her muff.

La Toilette du matin, Jean-Baptiste Chardin

Paysan et paysanne, by Étienne Aubrey.
This peasant family is wearing very simple clothes made of wool or cotton, perhaps hand-me-down or homemade.

The Encyclopédie

Denis Diderot, 1713-1784, painted by Jean-Honoré Fragonard

One of the most important works produced by the thinkers of the Enlightenment was the *Encyclopédie, ou Dictionnaire raisonné des sciences, des arts et des métiers*. The *Encyclopédie* was intended to contain the sum total of human knowledge, including a description of "the fundamental principles and the most essential details of every science and every art, whether liberal or mechanical." In charge of this monumental work was the French philosopher Denis Diderot, aided by the mathematician d'Alembert, and many of the important writers and philosophers of the day—Voltaire, Rousseau and Montesquieu among others. The *Encyclopédie* was seen as a threat by the authorities and banned, but Diderot continued to publish it in secret.

The first volume of the *Encyclopédie, ou Dictionnaire raisonné des sciences, des arts et des métiers* was published in 1751. By 1765, 17 volumes of text were finished, as well as 11 volumes of illustrations. Supplements were added until 1780.

The volumes of plates, or full-page illustrations, showing how scientific machines operated, how craftsmen did their work, illustrating all aspects of human activity, were an important part of the *Encyclopédie*.

The beginnings of the Industrial Revolution

In Britain, by the late 1700s, certain inventions had begun to revolutionize the way work was done. No longer did weavers depend on a single person with a spinning wheel to provide the wool or cotton threads so they could make cloth. Now there were machines that could spin up to 120 spindles at once, and the work was done in a factory instead of in someone's home. The perfection of the steam engine meant that engineers could build steam-powered machines that powered the spinning machines and looms of the textile manufacturers, enabling them to make more high-quality cloth faster, and ran locomotives that could carry all these goods to market so they could be sold. These technological developments began the change from a rural, farm-based society to an urban, industrial one. This particular revolution began in Great Britain, but in time it spread to the other European countries and America.

James Watt did not invent the steam engine, but his modifications to the existing model improved its performance. Instead of just back-and-forth motion, his machine produced rotary motion, which meant that factories no longer depended on water mills for their power.

The spinning jenny, invented by James Hargreaves in 1764, allowed one person to produce eight bobbins of spun wool or cotton at a time.

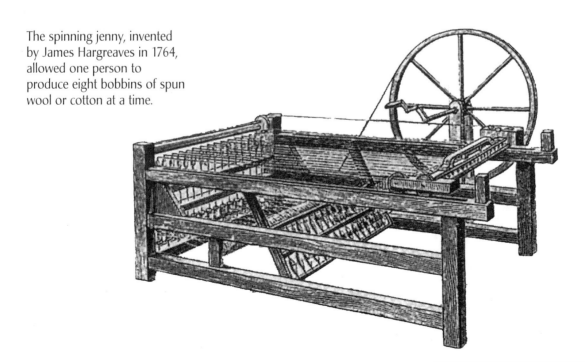

The Montgolfiers'
hot-air balloon

The steel-nibbed pen

The steam locomotive called
the "Catch-me-who-can."

Invention Timeline

1752   Lightning rods are invented to protect houses from fire caused by lightning strikes.

1762   The Earl of Sandwich demands a snack while playing cards. He is brought meat and cheese between two slices of bread, and a modern food staple is born.

1765   James Watt refines the steam engine, which will revolutionize British industry and transport.

1770   Porcelain false teeth are marketed.

1780   Samuel Harrison invents steel-nibbed pens to replace goose quill pens for writing.

1783   Man's first flight: the Montgolfier brothers fly their hot-air balloon.

1784   Benjamin Franklin, the American politician, philosopher and inventor, creates bifocal glasses.

1790   First sewing machine

1792   Dominique-Jean Larry, a French military surgeon, invents the horse-drawn ambulance as a more comfortable way to transport the wounded.

1793   Eli Whitney's cotton gin enables one person to do the work of 50 in the difficult job of cleaning raw cotton so it can be spun.

1796   Edward Jenner vaccinates patients against smallpox.

1800   The battery is invented by Alessandro Volta. Battery output is measured in volts.

1807   Gas lamps are installed in a London street.

1808   The "Catch-me-who-can", a steam locomotive, is built by Richard Trevithick, and raced against horses on a circular track to prove its superiority.

1811   The canning process for preserving food is invented in order to improve the quality of food in the French army.

1816   Putting his ear to a hollow tube on the patient's chest, French doctor René Laennec is able to hear the sounds of the heart and diagnose disease. This is the prototype of the stethoscope.

1820   With layers of gravel, crushed rock and tar, John McAdam modernizes road surfaces.

1823   Charles Mackintosh invents rubberized cloth for raincoats.

The Rococo style

Although we mark the change from Baroque music to Classical about 1750, changes in the visual arts began earlier than that. After the death of Louis XIV, in 1715, artistic fashion in France moved from the emotionally charged, heroic Baroque style to something lighter, more frivolous. This new style was not in opposition to Baroque, but really a modification of it. Called Rococo, after the French word *rocaille*, "rock-work," its decorative hallmark was the curved line, as found in sea-shells, flowers and sea-weed. Rococo was charming and elegant where Baroque was grand and majestic. Paris was the centre of this new style, but because all of Europe looked to France to see what the latest fashions were, Rococo spread all over the continent.

Interior of the Bavarian Church of the Wies

Rococo architecture

Rococo designers replaced the stateliness and grandeur of Baroque with smaller-scale grace and refinement. The huge halls of the previous period yielded to rooms that were more suitable for the elegant conversation that was one of society's main occupations. Pastel colours became more popular than majestic reds and purples, and buildings often seem intended simply to give pleasure, rather than to impress or terrify.

"The Princess's Salon" at the Parisian residence of the aristocratic Soubise family, c. 1740

The salon at the Hofburg Palace, Vienna, 1760–1780

Rococo painting

In contrast to the monumentally-sized works full of drama and emotion that were typical of the Baroque period, Rococo painters like Watteau, Boucher and Fragonard painted elegant men and women enjoying themselves. Most popular were scenes taken from the elegant outdoor entertainments that were called *fêtes galantes*. Instead of being found in the grip of a heroic struggle, their subjects dally in wooded glades singing of love. These were pictures designed to be hung in the home of a sophisticated member of the pleasure-loving French nobility, not the great halls of palaces.

The Swing, by Jean-Honoré Fragonard (1732–1806), appealed to the pleasure-seeking aristocrats who were at their height before the French Revolution.

A Pilgrimage to Cytheria, Jean-Antoine Watteau (1684–1721)

Watteau's masterpiece, painted in 1717, illustrates his world of love and gallantry. His delicate touch and the shimmering quality of his colour gave his work a dream-like quality.

The Music Lesson, François Boucher (1703–1770)

Boucher, greatly influenced by Watteau, was probably the most popular painter of his day, but has since been considered overly sentimental.

Rococo painting

Art works in the *fête galante* style prevailed in the Rococo period, but there was another significant painter at the time whose works were in sharp contrast to this almost frivolous style. Jean-Baptiste Siméon Chardin (1699–1779) found his inspiration in the lives of ordinary people and the things that surrounded them.

Le déjeuner, Chardin

Back from the Market, Chardin 1739

Kitchen Still Life, Chardin, c. 1731

Chardin seems to treat these simple objects with as much warmth and respect as he does the people who use them.

The Neoclassical style

Enlightenment ideas about the natural goodness of man and the importance of reason created a climate for change in art as well as politics. During the same time, archeological discoveries about ancient Greece and Rome were being made and written about. Greek democracy and the Roman republic were seen as models for the new age, and artists were inspired by the ideals of beauty expressed in the artworks of these societies. Rococo works were seen as trivial and silly compared with the ancients' simplicity and naturalness.

Osterly Park House, Middlesex, England, designed by Robert Adam

Neoclassical architecture

One of the places where these ideas first took expression was in Britain, through the Scottish architect Robert Adam. He introduced the neoclassical style by designing buildings according to proportions worked out by the Greeks and Romans. Adam also used classical-style columns and decorative work and became a very well known architect with a series of country houses in the 1750s and 1760s.

After the Revolution in France, architects there began to design buildings in the neoclassical style. When Napoleon came to power, he wanted to turn Paris into the new Rome. Two of the famous structures he commissioned are the *Arc de Triomphe*, and the church called *La Madeleine*.

Charlotte Square, New Town, Edinburgh, Robert Adam

The buildings in Charlotte Square are very simply decorated with columns and repeated round arches.

Architects in other countries were also swept up in the fascination for the classical style. The Brandenburg Gate in Berlin was modelled after a monumental gateway that was part of the ancient Greek citadel called the Acropolis, and Thomas Jefferson based the library called the Rotunda at the University of Virginia on the Pantheon, a famous Roman temple.

Neoclassical architecture

La Madeleine, Paris, Pierre Alexandre Vignon

Napoleon wanted the building to look like an ancient temple built to celebrate not a god or goddess, but himself and his empire.

The Arc de Triomphe du Carrousel

Napoleon actually built three Arcs de Triomphe. This first one was a copy of an arch in Rome, and originally had four bronze horses on top that were spoils of battle taken from Venice. The chariot and team you see in this picture were put there later, after the Venetians got their horses back in a later peace treaty.

The Brandenburg Gate, Berlin 1788–1791

The Rotunda, University of Virginia, 1819–1826

Neoclassical painting

The painter most characteristic of the neoclassical period is Jacques-Louis David (1748–1825). The revolutionary fervour of his patriotic works captures the stern morality that the times favoured. The leafy glades of the Rococo were gone, replaced by austere Roman heroes sacrificing everything for their country. David also painted many wonderful portraits, in which he put aside the high moral tone of his political paintings.

David's student, Jean-Auguste-Dominique Ingres, was the last neoclassical painter, leader of the neoclassical school opposed to the romantic movement.

The Oath of the Horatii, Jacques-Louis David, 1784. The three brothers swear an oath to fight for their city in spite of the sorrow this causes the women in the family.

The Death of Socrates, Jacques-Louis David, 1787

This illustration of ancient virtue shows the Greek philosopher Socrates, condemned to death for his opinions, on the point of drinking the poison hemlock.

The Apotheosis of Homer, J.A.D. Ingres, 1827
Here we see the Greek poet Homer as the father of poetry, being raised to the status of a God. He is surrounded by other literary figures Racine, Molière, Boileau and Shakespeare as well as the painters Raphael and Poussin. Apparently Ingres considered including Mozart in the painting, but decided otherwise because he thought that music was too impermanent an art for this revered company.

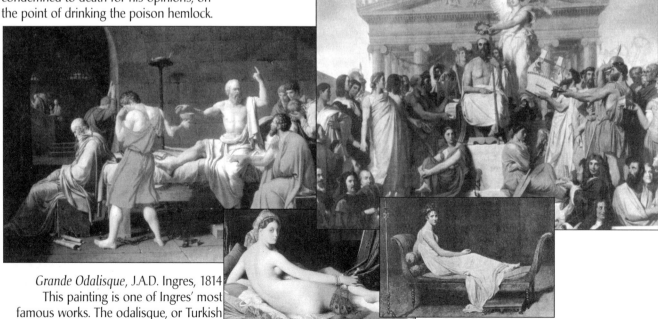

Grande Odalisque, J.A.D. Ingres, 1814
This painting is one of Ingres' most famous works. The odalisque, or Turkish slave, is not a typical neoclassical subject, but he has painted her according to neoclassical principles.

Madame Récamier, Jacques-Louis David, 1800. Madame Récamier is painted as though she were a Greek statue. Note all the elements of neoclassical style – the pose, the dress, the bench, the absolute naturalness of the bare feet.

Neoclassical sculpture

Neoclassical sculptors moved away from the dramatic, emotional forms that were typical of the Baroque period towards more idealized classical poses. The Italian Antonio Canova was perhaps the leading neoclassical sculptor of his day. Napoleon commissioned him to make statues of himself and his family.

Napoleon's sister Pauline as Venus, goddess of love, reclining

Jean-Antoine Houdon was the most important portrait sculptor of the entire Classical period, and he is not as easy to classify as Canova. His sculptures show real character, not just an idealized vision of his subject in classical drapery. His work includes busts and statues of many Enlightenment thinkers, like Diderot, Rousseau and Voltaire. He also did portraits of many heroes of the American Revolution.

Napoleon, Antonio Canova, 1802–1810

Voltaire, J.-A. Houdon, 1781. Houdon uses the drapery to link Voltaire with the Greek philosophers, and suggests his famous intelligence and wit with a look of amused skepticism.

George Washington, J.-A. Houdon, 1788–92
Jefferson invited Houdon to come to America to make a statue of George Washington, the country's first president. Houdon portrays him as a decent country gentleman called to his country's service, a model right out of Republican Rome, without the toga.

Breaking away from patronage

During the Baroque era, almost all musicians worked under what is known as the patronage system. That means that they worked in the court of a king or another member of the aristocracy, or for the church, and they produced whatever music their employers needed. It was very difficult to earn a living as a musician any other way. It was difficult in the Classical period as well, but times were changing. When we look at the careers of the three most important composers of the era, Haydn, Mozart and Beethoven, we can see the ways in which each of them broke with the system.

St. Michael's Square in Vienna, showing the Burgtheater in the centre. It was typical of the concert halls where composers becoming more independent during the Classical era could have their works performed.

Haydn's career was the most traditional. For 30 years, he worked for the Princes Esterházy, living primarily in their palaces and being responsible for all the music they required. Still, he changed the system in small ways. He managed to get permission to earn money from publishing his music when traditionally the employer had all the rights to a composer's work. And towards the end of his life, he was able to travel and live on his own, composing works on commission for other people, and writing music in order to publish it. Mozart began his career working for a prince of the church, but rebelled against the system and struck out on his own. He didn't want to be told what to write, so he composed works for concerts he himself would put on for the public and he composed works on commission. It was a risky, hand-to-mouth existence. Beethoven was supported by rich patrons, but they did not tell him what to write. He was able to compose as he wanted and perform in concerts to raise money. He also earned money by publishing his music, sometimes selling the rights to more than one publishing house!

The rise of the public concert

A larger and more prosperous middle class meant that there were more people in the society who were interested in music and had the money to pay for it. Some were rich enough to employ musicians as aristocrats did, but those with less money could afford to go to public concerts. They could buy tickets for individual concerts or a subscription for a whole series. Concerts were also staged as charity fund-raisers. In time, orchestras began to be formed and kept together as a team, rather than hired (on a piece-meal basis) every time there was a concert. Newspapers began to advertise concerts, and even send someone to write a critique of the performance that they would publish.

With the establishment of the Conservatory of Music in Paris after the Revolution came the first attempt to define the musical canon, the body of music from the past and present that all musicians ought to know.

Public concerts in the Classical period were quite different from the ones we have now. For one thing, they were a lot longer. Usually an orchestra performed one or two symphonies, although these were rarely played straight though — often they saved the last movement for a rousing finish. Vocal works would have been included, sung by members of the local opera company, as well as a concerto. When Mozart gave a concert, he would include an improvisation, where he would amuse the audience by playing variations on a popular theme.

The interior of an opera house in France in the 1700s

Unlike us, audiences in the Classical period expected to hear all new work at every concert, which explains the massive output of a composer like Haydn, who had to write music for every entertainment at court. Beethoven was among the first composers who thought his work ought to have such an impact that people would want to hear the music again.

An ad for a concert in Boston, Massachusetts, in 1769

A ticket for a concert in London in 1799, designed by the famous painter William Hogarth. Notice how elaborately decorated the ticket is.

The developing market for music at home

Musical accomplishment, especially the ability to play the piano, was regarded as an important social asset for women.

The rise of the middle class also meant that many more people wanted to make music themselves. They wanted lessons, and they wanted music they could play. Composers often chose to write the kind of music that could be played by a small ensemble of amateur musicians, because they knew there were plenty of people who would buy the published music. They would also make arrangements of some of their works, so that compositions that had begun as symphonies or concertos in the concert hall could be rewritten for piano or for string quartet. It was not illegal to use someone else's work without asking, as it is nowadays, and some musicians made money by arranging the compositions of others. Mozart's father told him to get arrangements of his music out quickly, so he would get the money before someone else did. In addition, once composers sold their work to a publisher, that was all the income they could expect from it. All the profits from selling the published pieces would be kept by the publisher. Now a publisher has to pay a certain percentage of the work's selling price to the composer for every copy sold.

A private house concert

Clear, accessible music

Music was becoming a source of entertainment to more and more people. Composers had to appeal to the broader public, because many more people were becoming involved with music, either as concertgoers or home musicians. They wanted music to be less complex to listen to and easier to play, music that was lighter, clearer and more accessible. Balance and proportion were important to them. One of the ways composers achieved these goals was by using short phrases that occur in regular patterns. Another was to write lyrical melodies accompanied by chords. These chords were emerging from the major/minor key system that had been developing throughout the Baroque period and was now much more clearly understood.

George, Third Earl of Cowper, and the Gore Family, by Johann Zoffany, shows a group of aristocrats making music. The square piano was very commonly found in homes in the late 1700s.

Short balanced phrases

Classical composers favoured two- or four-bar phrases instead of the typical long lines found in Baroque music. Look at this illustration of the first line from Mozart's *A Little Night Music*. You can see that the first phrase contains two bars, and the notes generally seem to go up. The second two bars are almost the same, except that the notes go down. It is as though the first phrase is opening and the second is closing. This kind of balance makes the patterns in the music easy for the listener to understand.

A Little Night Music, Mozart

Repetitions and signposts

Composers in the Classical era strove for clarity. **Themes**, for instance, are introduced, then repeated again immediately so that the audience becomes familiar with them, and repeated again later in the piece. As well, Classical composers built in signposts to tell the listeners where the music was going. As a way of leading into a theme, they often used little transitional phrases called **bridge passages** that suggest that something important is coming up. Closing off a theme was just as important. **Cadences** are sequences of notes or chords that seem to close a musical section and composers of this period often repeated the chords in the cadences many times to tell the audience that they were finished talking about one idea and were going to begin talking about something else.

A **theme** is a musical idea, a tune that forms the basis of a musical composition.

A **bridge passage** is a musical link between two important sections of a composition. It often includes a change of key.

A **cadence** is a melodic or a harmonic formula that ends a work, or a section of a work, or a phrase, and suggests that it brings a conclusion.

An example of a final cadence, this one from Clementi's Sonatina, op.36, no.3

Lyrical melodies with harmonic accompaniment

The word **texture** refers to the way the different lines of the music fit together. In the Renaissance and Baroque periods, the prevailing texture was that of several melodies woven together. This is called **polyphony**. Melody with harmonic accompaniment is the predominant texture of the music written in the Classical era. This kind of music is called **homophony**.

Classical composers wrote elegant, lyrical lines of music and the harmonies acted like vertical columns of sound holding up the melodies. The polyphony of Baroque composers was not abandoned completely, but it was not as commonly used. This change in favour of homophony was one of the most momentous changes in musical history, because melody and accompaniment remained the prevailing texture of serious Western music until well into the 1900s, and continues to be the basis for most popular music such as jazz, rock and pop.

The French philosopher Jean-Jacques Rousseau, complaining about polyphony, said that listening to four lines of music played at the same time makes as much sense as listening to four people talking at once.

Texture describes the way the individual notes in the music are blended together.

Polyphony is a texture in which several independent lines of music are woven together.

Homophony is a texture in which the melodic line leads and is supported by a chordal accompaniment.

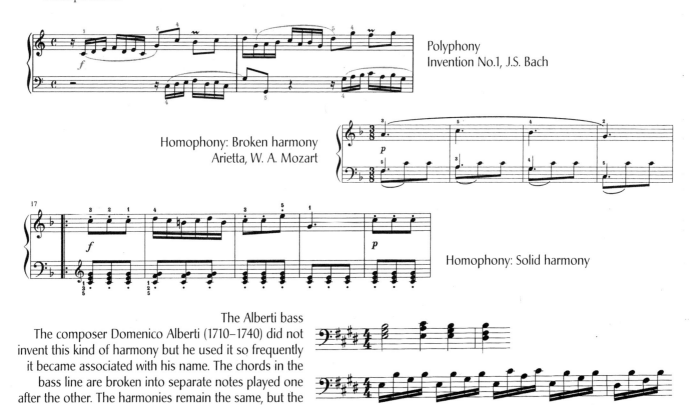

Polyphony
Invention No.1, J.S. Bach

Homophony: Broken harmony
Arietta, W. A. Mozart

Homophony: Solid harmony

The Alberti bass
The composer Domenico Alberti (1710–1740) did not invent this kind of harmony but he used it so frequently it became associated with his name. The chords in the bass line are broken into separate notes played one after the other. The harmonies remain the same, but the broken chords add a sense of movement and lightness.

More flexible rhythm

First motif

Classical composers thought that the driving, unchanging rhythm common to the Baroque period was boring. They preferred to write music with greater variety. Look at this illustration of the notes that make up the motifs that Mozart used in the first movement of his Symphony no.40 in G Minor. The first motif is made up largely of quarter and eighth notes all grouped the same way, and the second has contrasting longer and shorter notes, like dotted half notes and sixteenths. This kind of variation avoided the unflagging predictability of Baroque music.

Second motif

Dynamics

During the Baroque period, instrumental music tended to be played at a constant level of loudness and softness. Classical composers wanted to add more variety to the volume at which their music was played. They planned that particular passages would be played at specific volumes, and it was during this period that scores began to have dynamic marks like *pp*, or *mf*, added to them, so that performers would know exactly what volume the composer wanted.

Crescendos (growing louder) and decrescendos (getting softer) also began to be written into the music during the Classical period and they added a great deal of excitement. Performers wanted their music to grow louder and softer within a single passage, the way a singer's voice can, and they began varying the dynamics more and more, shaping the different melodies they played.

Dynamic Marks		
pp = pianissimo, very soft	*mp* = mezzo piano, moderately soft	*f* = forte, loud
p = piano, soft	*mf* = mezzo forte, moderately loud	*ff* = fortissimo, very loud
Crescendo mark ⟨		*Diminuendo/Decrescendo* mark ⟩

Theme and variations

In this form, composers begin with one theme, or melodic idea, and then write a series of pieces which all modify the original theme in different ways. They can vary the melody by adding or subtracting notes. They can change the key, the harmony or the rhythms, or repeat the melody with different music around it. Often composers used this form to show off their skill at improvising to entertain people at a party or during a concert. They would be given a theme, and they would improvise as many variations as they could right then and there. These improvisations were often written down later and published. One famous example of theme and variations form is the series of variations that Mozart improvised on the French folk tune called "Ah, vous dirai-je Maman" which we know as "Twinkle, Twinkle, Little Star."

Minuet and trio

In the Baroque period, composers developed a kind of composition called a suite, which was made up of many different types of dance music. Classical composers took one particular type of dance music, the minuet, and incorporated it into many different kinds of compositions. The minuet was a stately dance in 3/4 time, and the minuet and trio form was composed of two separate minuets, one used for the first and last sections, and the other for the middle section. The first minuet, **A**, was followed by a second, **B**. Then **A** was repeated, to give an **A-B-A** structure to the piece. The **B** section was always called a trio because it was originally played by three instruments. It generally presents a contrast to the **A** sections, using a different key, different instruments or different rhythms. Symphonies in the Classical period often had a minuet as the third movement.

Rondo

A rondo is a form in which the main musical idea keeps coming back. Composers during the Classical era usually introduced the first theme **A**, then moved to a second **B**, went back to the first **A** before adding a third theme **C**. They would repeat theme **A** after every new theme, and end with it as well. You can think of the rondo form then as **A-B-A-C-A-D-A**. The rondo is often used as the last movement of a symphony or other large work. One of the most famous rondos is the *Turkish Rondo* from Mozart's Piano Sonata in A Major.

First movement form

First-movement form, also known as sonata form, or sonata-allegro form, was developed in the Classical period and became the form most frequently used by composers of the era. The most important thing about this form is the conflict between two keys, and it is this conflict and its resolution that provide the dramatic effect. First-movement form can be divided into two sections. In the first, the music is established in one key, called the home key, and then moves to a contrasting key. In the second section, the composer plays around with those two keys, introducing other keys as well, and then brings us back to the home key. The drama can be heightened by using different **thematic groups** in the home key and in the contrasting key. Dramatic contrast can also be added using different registers, different dynamic levels and different rhythmic structures.

First-movement form was a development of the old two-section structure of the Baroque sonata, and it became the basis for much of the music written in the Classical period, primarily used as the first movement of symphonies, concertos and sonatas. During the Romantic period, first-movement form continued to be popular and evolved into a three-part structure, made up of exposition, development and recapitulation, but current research suggests that the two-section analysis is a more accurate representation of what was really taking place in the Classical period.

A **thematic group** is made up of several motifs, or short melodies, in the same key which function together in the same section of a form.

First movement form

FIRST SECTION   SECOND SECTION

***** : || ||

| First thematic group in home key | Bridge | Second thematic group in contrasting key | Series of cadences in contrasting key | Some new, some old material in different keys | Move into home key with previous thematic groups | Cadences in home key |

The above diagram may help to explain this very important concept. The first section begins with the first thematic group in the home key. Then there is a transition passage, or bridge, presenting new thematic material, often reused later on, which moves the music into the contrasting key. The composer then introduces the second thematic group in the contrasting key, which may include some old thematic material as well as some new, and emphasizes the idea of that contrasting key with a series of cadences.

The second section serves to work out the conflict established in the first section between the two keys. First, new and old thematic material in various keys is presented. Then the music moves back into the home key. While composers sometimes bring back the first thematic group at this point, they always bring back the second thematic group. This time, however, it is in the home key, which gives the music a sense that the conflict has been resolved. Then another series of cadences in the home key follow, to underscore that feeling of resolution.

None of this was carved in stone, of course, and Classical composers worked out the structure differently with each piece they wrote.

Opera

The most common kind of opera at the beginning of the Classical period was the *opera seria*, or tragic Italian opera. Such operas dealt with mythological heroes or kings and queens, and consisted mainly of arias, highly emotional songs for solo voice. The stars of *opera seria* were the sopranos, the women with the highest voices, and the castrati, men whose voices had never broken and who still sang in the soprano and alto registers.

The characters in comic operas were often hiding and then being caught out. Here a page boy is discovered hiding under a dress that the maid-servant has laid over a chair..

However, during the Classical era when the doctrine of natural man was evolving, people found this kind of opera artificial; they wanted operas about ordinary people, not mythological heros. They wanted emotions more realistically portrayed, and singers who did not draw all the attention to themselves and away from the story. For this they turned to comic opera, which had different names in different countries. In Italy it was called *opera buffa*, in France *opéra comique*, in England *ballad opera*, and in Germany *Singspiel*. It had a number of features that made it extremely popular with audiences.

Some of this popularity was because comic operas were written in the language spoken by the audience, instead of the traditional Italian of *opera seria*, which very few could understand. The naturalness of spoken dialogue, which was used between arias and vocal ensembles in all types but the Italian *opera buffa*, added to audience's ready acceptance of the genre. In addition, the characters were real people, not gods and goddesses, and the stories were told with a great deal of humour and lots of silly situations. A new emphasis was placed on the bass voice in the form of the buffo, the comic male character. Instead of the long, drawn-out arias of *opera seria*, comic operas had ensemble numbers at the end of each act that brought all the soloists together and provided a great deal of excitement. Mozart wrote several comic operas, including *The Marriage of Figaro*, and *Così Fan Tutti* (Women Are Like That). His genius lifted the *opera buffa* to a higher plane.

Opera

TRAGIC OPERA (OPERA SERIA)	COMIC OPERA (OPERA BUFFA)
Gods and goddesses, kings and queens Series of arias, highly emotional solos Choicest roles went to sopranos, male or female Serious stories	Ordinary people Music no longer just a showcase for the soloists, more ensemble pieces Good parts for bass voice, the buffo, comic male role Silly situations, humorous dialogue

The sopranos were the real stars of the opera, not the composers. They made a great deal of money, and had large numbers of adoring fans. This is Nancy Storace, one of the famous sopranos of the Classical era.

In this picture, Mozart is shown accompanying the soprano Caterina Cavalieri.

Here is a performance of one of Gluck's operas at the theatre at Schönbrunn Palace in Vienna.

Choral music

Choral music, both sacred (religious in nature) and secular (non-religious), was very important in the Baroque period, and Classical composers continued the tradition. The main forms of sacred choral music were the mass, the requiem and the oratorio.

A mass, in musical terms, is the music written for the Roman Catholic church service. A requiem is the music written for a mass for the dead. The oratorio is an opera-like retelling of stories from the Bible with choir, soloists and orchestra, but without costumes or scenery. All the well-known composers of the Classical period wrote sacred choral music. Haydn wrote 15 masses and three oratorios, of which *The Creation* is the most famous. Mozart wrote 15 masses as well, including the requiem he was working on when he died. Beethoven's *Missa solemnis* (Mass in D) is one of his greatest works.

The piano

During the Baroque period, the harpsichord was the most popular keyboard instrument. Then, just before the beginning of the Classical period, a new keyboard instrument, the pianoforte or fortepiano, was introduced. It quickly overtook the harpsichord in popularity.

The way the two instruments produce sound is very different. In the harpsichord, hitting a key causes a mechanism to pluck a string. With the piano, a leather-headed hammer strikes the string. The harpsichord's plucked strings mean the volume of a sound remains constant, no matter how hard the keys are struck. Pianos, however, produce soft or loud sounds depending on the force of the touch. Musicians began to realize that the pianoforte could produce the exciting crescendos and decrescendos that they and their audiences wanted to hear.

The harpsichord is characterized by a crisp and bright sound which decays quickly. As the pianoforte evolved, it developed quite a different sound quality, a smoother, more sustained sound that resonated for a longer time.

Mozart's fortepiano, now on display at the Mozarteum in Salzburg

The early pianoforte was much softer than a modern-day piano. By Beethoven's time, the instrument was already much louder and stronger, although still not capable of producing as much sound as it is now. Nevertheless, the pianoforte was clearly better suited to the concert hall.

At first, musicians simply transferred their harpsichord technique to the new instrument, and composers published their music for either one. But Mozart, Clementi and, later on, Beethoven developed a new keyboard technique that made use of the fortepiano's ability to vary the dynamics and produce **cantabile** and **legato** effects. Mozart's concertos, Clementi's sonatas and all of Beethoven's keyboard works were written specially for the pianoforte and were no longer appropriate for the harpsichord.

A square piano manufactured at the Clementi piano factory in London, 1824

Cantabile means in a singing style. **Legato** means smoothly connected.

The orchestra

The orchestra during the Baroque period consisted mainly of strings: two groups of violins, violas, cellos and a few basses. There was always a keyboard instrument, either harpsichord or organ, and sometimes flutes, oboes, bassoons and trumpets might be added.

In the Classical orchestra, the strings still occupied a predominant place, and their number depended on the wealth of the orchestra's sponsor. There might be as many as twelve first violinists and twelve seconds, six violists, eight cellists and four basses. On the other hand, some orchestras managed with only three or four first violins, the same number of seconds, two violas, two cellos and only one bass.

The keyboard instrument, however, lost its orchestral role, because it was no longer needed to play the continuous bass part that played such an important role in Baroque music. Another change was that the woodwind and brass sections were given a more important role within the orchestra and as solo instruments. Clarinets were now added to the wind section because the new, improved clarinet was able to stay in tune throughout its full range. French horns were the mainstay of the brass section, although trumpets were sometimes used too. As for the percussion section, the only kind of drums used were timpani, or kettle drums, unless a Turkish sound was wanted. If so, cymbals, triangle and bass drum would be added. There was a certain fascination with Turkey at the time and composers often added sounds influenced by Turkish music to get an exotic effect. Mozart did so in his comic opera *The Abduction from the Seraglio*, as did Haydn in his "Military" Symphony, and Beethoven in his Symphony No. 9.

The orchestra

Wind instruments provide sounds in various registers: flutes, clarinets and oboes make high sounds, bassoons, low ones. The brass instruments are in the middle range. These instruments could be added to the strings when the composer wanted more volume. As well, each type of instrument added its own particular colour of sound. Composers carefully combined the different colours of sound to get the effects they wanted.

It was written at the time, "No orchestra in the world has ever excelled the Mannheim one. Its *forte* is a thunderclap, its *crescendo* a cataract, its *diminuendo* a crystal stream bubbling in the distance, its *piano* a breath of spring."

THE EARLY CLASSICAL ORCHESTRA

Strings	Woodwinds	Brass	Percussion
First violins	2 Flutes	2 French horns	2 Timpani
Second violins	2 Oboes	2 Trumpets*	
Violas	2 Clarinets*		
Cellos	2 Bassoons		
Bass viols		*Optional	

A musician surrounded by instruments in a neoclassical setting

Virtuoso orchestras

The new music being written for orchestras required a very high level of playing, and some orchestras began to gain a reputation for their skill. One particularly famous one in Mannheim, Germany, played such exciting crescendos that a writer of the time reported that "audiences would rise in their seats as the music grew louder." This one orchestra influenced the way music was written and played all over Europe.

The symphony

The origins of the symphony lie in the overtures, or introductory orchestral music, written for Italian opera during the Baroque period. These *sinfonia*, as they were called in Italian, really had nothing that connected them with the operas that followed them, and they soon began to be played by themselves, in concerts. The idea caught on, and composers began writing symphonies that were completely independent of operas. In the hands of composers like Haydn and Mozart, the symphony became the crowning glory of the Classical period.

Originally a work in three sections, fast-slow-fast, the symphony became a four-movement work. The first movement was always an Allegro, a fast tempo, written in the first-movement form we discussed earlier. The second movement was usually a slow and lyrical three-part form, the third often a minuet and trio in a moderate tempo, and the fourth a faster and lighter movement, often in first-movement or rondo form.

THE SYMPHONY

Movement	Form	Tempo
First movement	1st movement form	Allegro (fast)
Second movement	Three-part form (ABA)	Slow
Third movement	Minuet and trio	Moderate
Fourth movement	1st movement or rondo form	Fast

Chamber music

Chamber music is written for small ensembles and designed to be played, as its name suggests, in a smaller place than would be required for a full orchestra. This kind of music may be written for various instruments in duets (groups of two) trios (three), quartets (four), quintets (five) and even more. Large ensembles were possible: Beethoven wrote a septet (seven) for winds, and Mozart an octet (eight) also for winds, but the most common combination of instruments was the string quartet.

A string quartet contains four instruments: two violins, a viola and a cello. This provides a balance of high and low registers, and since they all belong to the same family of instruments, they fit together perfectly. The music written for string quartet tends to follow the same four-movement and tempo pattern as the symphony. Mozart composed 30 string quartets, Beethoven 16, and Haydn 67.

A string quartet: two violins, viola and cello

A Court Concert at Liège, by P. J. Delcloche, 1755

Here we see a chamber orchestra rehearsing.

The concerto

The Baroque concerto was based on the contrast between a solo instrument or solo group and the rest of the orchestra. As the concerto developed in the Classical period, more emphasis was placed on the solo instrument, particularly piano or violin. The virtuosity of the soloist was now pitted against a more powerful orchestra with a greater variety of sound colours.

Classical concertos were generally three-movement works on a fast-slow-fast pattern. They included a new feature near the end of the piece called a cadenza, where the orchestra stopped playing and the soloist, most often the composer himself, showed off his virtuoso talents.

Piano and violin concertos were very common during the Classical period. Mozart wrote five violin and 27 piano concertos, while Beethoven wrote five for piano and one for violin. Other instruments had concertos written for them as well. Mozart's Horn Concerto in E flat and his Clarinet Concerto in A are two of his most famous.

The sonata

Piano sonatas were written for solo piano, and violin or cello sonatas were written for either of these instruments accompanied by piano. Sometimes composers wrote sonatas so they could perform the music themselves, but often sonatas were intended for performances on a much smaller scale, for amateurs at home. Because there was such a demand for pieces that amateurs could play, an enormous amount of sonata music was written. They were generally in three movements in alternating tempos, like concertos.

This engraving, dating from 1773, shows two people playing a violin sonata. As was typical at the time, the man is the violinist and the woman is accompanying him on the keyboard. Women were much less likely to play the violin than a keyboard instrument.

The Music Lesson,
Jean-Honoré Fragonard

Carl Philipp Emmanuel Bach (1714–1788)

The most famous of Johann Sebastian Bach's musician sons, C. P. E. Bach was the leading keyboard player of his era. He was harpsichordist to Frederick the Great of Prussia for thirty years, and music director for the city of Hamburg, in what is now Germany, after that. He composed a great deal of keyboard music in particular in an intermediate style between Baroque and Classical. In fact, he is often called a pre-Classical composer. During his lifetime, his music was much more popular than his father's and he was a major influence on the development of first-movement form in the Classical period. His book, *Essay on the True Art of Playing Keyboard Instruments*, is still an important reference work for musicians interested in the keyboard repertoire of the period. His works were carefully studied by all three Classical masters, Haydn, Mozart and Beethoven. Mozart said of C. P. E. Bach, "He is the father, and we are all the children."

Carl Philipp Emmanuel Bach

The artist is doing a portrait of two men – the one standing in the centre is C.P.E. Bach.

Johann Stamitz (1717–1757)

Stamitz was the conductor of the famous Mannheim orchestra, and responsible for a great deal of the symphony's early development. He wrote more than 70 symphonies, and changed the fast-slow-fast pattern to a four–movement plan that became standard for the Classical symphony. His innovations include an increase in dynamic contrast, introducing contrasting themes in the same movement, eliminating the continuous bass, and increasing the use of wind instruments. He was an influential teacher—Johann Christian Bach, another of Johann Sebastian's famous sons, was one of his students. In addition to the symphonies, he composed concertos for violin, clarinet, flute, oboe and harpsichord, chamber music and church music.

Christoph Willibald Gluck (1714–1787)

Gluck is the composer most responsible for producing a new kind of opera that reflected the changing times and ideas in the Classical period. He believed that opera should convey emotions more naturally and truthfully than did the heroics of the *opera seria*. Traditionally arias were designed primarily to show off the singers' voices, but Gluck wrote arias that suited the story of the opera. He also assigned important roles to the chorus, and his operas have wonderful examples of choral scenes and dances. He wrote over forty operas, the best known being *Orpheus and Eurydice* (1762), the ancient Greek story of Orpheus's voyage to Hades, the home of the dead, to recover his wife, Eurydice.

Frontispiece to the first edition of Gluck's *Orpheus and Eurydice* published in Paris in 1764.

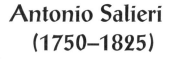

Antonio Salieri (1750–1825)

Salieri was born in Italy but spent most of his working life in Vienna. He was primarily a composer of operas in the Italian style, and was music director to the court of the Emperor of Austria for 36 years. He was a protege of Gluck, and had some success with his operas until he virtually retired from composing at the age of 54, saying that musical tastes were turning away from his kind of music. He composed over 40 operas, four oratorios, a great deal of church music and many vocal and instrumental pieces. He was an important teacher and his list of pupils includes Beethoven, Schubert and Liszt. He and Mozart were rivals, and there is a certain amount of evidence that he prevented the performance of some of Mozart's works. Their relationship was generally cordial, however.

This picture shows Gluck presenting one of his scores to Marie Antoinette, the Queen of France.

Muzio Clementi (1752–1832)

Muzio Clementi

Clementi was Italian, but he worked mainly in London. He is primarily remembered for his keyboard compositions, and his collection of 100 studies of increasing difficulty, *Gradus ad Parnassum*, is still used to teach good piano technique. His compositions also include many sonatas and sonatinas, duets and variations. In addition to his work as a composer, Clementi founded a music publishing house and a piano factory.

Johann Nepomuk Hummel (1778–1837)

Hummel studied in Vienna under Mozart, Salieri, Clementi and Haydn. He was second kapellmeister, or assistant music director, under Haydn to Prince Esterházy from 1804 to 1811. He toured extensively as a pianist, and composed both church and chamber music, operas, and ballets, as well as seven piano concertos. His piano method was published in 1828. His writing for piano influenced Chopin.

Friedrick Kuhlau (1786–1832)

Friedrick Kuhlau was a German-born pianist and composer who worked at the court of Denmark. He is best known for his keyboard compositions, which include a concerto and many teaching pieces. Many piano students will be familiar with his sonatinas. He also composed six operas and other stage music, as well as chamber music, much of it for flute.

Maddalena Laura Lombardini Sirmen
(1745–1818)

Maddalena Lombardini was an Italian composer, violinist and singer. At the age of seven, she auditioned for and won a place at the *ospedale* music school run by a religious order in Venice, where she studied violin, singing and solfège. By the age of 14, she had been promoted to violin teacher. She married Ludovico Sirmen, another violinist, and together they toured Italy, Paris and London. She performed her own violin concertos, and also sang various operatic roles. She was appointed first woman singer at the Imperial Theatre in St. Petersburg, Russia. Lombardini Sirmen's work as a composer was highly regarded and her published compositions were available all over Europe. Best known are the violin concertos, but her six string quartets are also important.

Maddalena Lombardini
Sirmen

Maria Theresia von Paradis
(1759–1824)

The daughter of Austrian Imperial Court Secretary Josef von Paradis, and named for the Austrian Empress, Maria Theresia von Paradis was trained for a career in music. Although she became blind at the age of three, she studied piano, singing and composition with some of the most important Viennese musicians of her time. At the age of 24 she began a successful three-year tour of Europe. After she returned to Vienna, she spent more time composing, using a pegboard system invented for her by a friend. Although she continued to perform until she was 50, one of her major interests was the music school for girls she established in 1808. Their Sunday concerts were popular with Viennese society. She wrote several operas, other vocal works, two piano concertos and several other keyboard works, but most of the scores have been lost.

Family background and musical education

This is the thatched cottage where Haydn was born in Lower Austria. He had two brothers and three sisters, and both of his brothers also became musicians.

Joseph Haydn was born in a modest home in the village of Rohrau, about 30 miles outside of Vienna, Austria. Haydn's father made wheels for carts and carriages, but he loved music, and often sang and accompanied himself on the harp. Young Joseph learned to sing his father's songs, and his beautiful voice was noticed by his uncle, Johann Franck, a schoolmaster. Franck suggested that Joseph should come to his school and sing in the parish church choir. So at the age of six, Haydn left home.

While he was at his uncle's school, the choirmaster of St. Stephen's Cathedral in Vienna heard him sing, and was so impressed with his ability that he asked the boy, who was then eight years old, to come and study at the choir school attached to the Cathedral. Vienna was one of the most important musical centres in the world in those days, so it was a very great opportunity.

The choirboys at St. Stephen's had to sing at two church services every day, as well as for weddings, funerals and other special occasions. Their education consisted of religion, Latin, mathematics and writing, plus studies in singing, violin and harpsichord. When his voice began to break, Haydn was dismissed from the choir and he had to try and make a living as a freelance musician.

The choirboys at St. Stephen's often performed at the Schönbrunn Palace for the Empress Maria Theresa. Here she is shown with her family at the Palace.

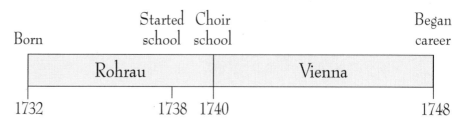

Born	Started school	Choir school	Began career
Rohrau		Vienna	
1732	1738	1740	1748

Hard times and modest success

Haydn was very poor, and he took almost any job he could find. He bought himself an old harpsichord, did a little teaching, sang as a tenor in a nearby church, and played violin at parties and private concerts. During this difficult time he studied music theory on his own, and learned a great deal by working through the keyboard sonatas of C. P. E. Bach. He took some lessons from the well-known Italian singing master and composer, Nicola Porpora, and became his accompanist, and at times his personal servant. Haydn credited Porpora with teaching him the fundamentals of composition

Haydn and his wife, Maria Anna Keller, at the time of their marriage

Through Porpora, Haydn began to meet wealthy Austrian noblemen who commissioned him to compose for them, and in 1759 he obtained his first salaried position, as music director to Count Morzin. During this period, Haydn married Maria Anna Keller, the daughter of a wigmaker. Haydn's wife was not interested in music and never really valued his work. The marriage did not turn out well and they never had any children.

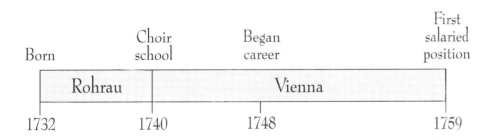

	Choir school	Began career	First salaried position
Born			
Rohrau		Vienna	
1732	1740	1748	1759

Appointment to the court of the Esterházys

Haydn as a young man

In 1761, Haydn accepted the position of assistant music director at the court of Prince Paul Anton Esterházy, one of the richest noblemen in Hungary. The Esterházys were great patrons of the arts, and Haydn stayed in the service of the Esterházy family for almost thirty years. He worked for four Esterházy princes, Prince Paul Anton, Prince Nikolaus, Prince Anton, and Prince Nikolaus II, in turn.

Prince Paul Anton Esterházy Employed Haydn from 1761 to 1762	Prince Nikolaus I, «Nikolaus the Magnificent» (brother of Paul Anton) Employed Haydn from 1762 to 1790
	Prince Anton Esterházy (son) Employed Haydn from 1790 to 1794
	Prince Nikolaus II (son) Employed Haydn from 1794 to 1809

The Esterházy castle at Eisenstadt

Haydn was first based at the Esterházy's castle at Eisenstadt, Austria. Musicians were still regarded as servants in those days, and Haydn was given a salary, and provided with a room and given his meals at the servants' table. He had to compose anything the Prince required, rehearse the orchestra and take care of the music and the instruments. In addition, Prince Paul Anton owned the rights to all Haydn's compositions. The Prince did not live long enough to enjoy much of Haydn's music, however. He died within a year of Haydn's arrival and was succeeded by his brother, Prince Nikolaus.

It was written into his first contract that he must wear the uniform of a court officer, wear a wig or powder and braid his hair, maintain standards of morality and sobriety, and avoid vulgarity in eating, drinking or speaking.

Born	Choir school	Began career	First salaried position	Begins work for Esterházys
Rohrau		Vienna		Eisenstadt
1732	1740	1748	1759	1761

Serving Prince Nikolaus

Prince Nikolaus I, the second Esterházy prince who employed Haydn, was called Nikolaus the Magnificent because he loved festivities and making a show. After returning from a trip to Paris and seeing Versailles, the fabulous palace of the King of France, he was determined to create a showplace of his own. On the site of his summer residence, he built a splendid palace which he called Esterháza. The palace had 126 guest rooms, a ballroom and a concert hall, magnificent gardens, and later, an opera house that seated 400 people. The palace was built in only two years, even though the land was boggy and had to be drained, and cost the Prince 11 million florins, or about $60 million in today's dollars.

Prince Nikolaus the Magnificent

For eleven years after Esterháza was built, Prince Nikolaus maintained his court there for nine or ten months a year. Sometimes the court musicians, who were not allowed to bring their families with them, found the long months on Esterháza's remote and dreary marshes rather difficult. Instead of speaking directly to the Prince on their behalf, Haydn wrote what has become known as the "Farewell" symphony. During the finale of the last movement, the musicians began to leave the stage: the oboes first, then the horns, bassoons and basses, and finally the strings in pairs, until only Haydn and one violinist were left. One version of the story has the musicians blowing out the candles on their music stands as they left, leaving the prince and the audience in darkness. Whether or not that part of the story is true, the prince apparently took the hint and the court was ordered to move back to Eisenstadt immediately.

Haydn was not always very happy about spending so much time at Esterhazá, away from the musical life of Vienna. Nevertheless, it is possible that Haydn's isolated situation had a good effect on the music he wrote. He himself said that without the influence of other people's music, he had no option but to become an original.

The Palace of Esterháza

Orchestral and vocal responsibilities

Haydn was originally hired to provide more orchestral and opera music at the court. However, in the early years, Haydn composed mostly instrumental music. The orchestra at his service initially had between ten and fifteen musicians, and they must have been good ones, because Haydn wrote several concertos in those first years, and concertos require musicians who are able to play the solo parts. He composed symphonies and concertos for twice-weekly concerts as well as for special events. He also wrote lighter works, divertimentos and minuets, purely for entertainment.

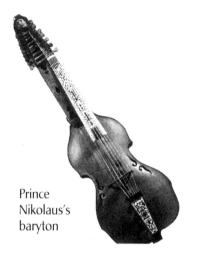

Prince Nikolaus's baryton

Prince Nikolaus played an instrument called the baryton, a string instrument with a set of extra strings that resonated when the main strings were played and could be plucked for a special effect. He requested that Haydn compose music for him to play, and Haydn obliged with over 125 trios for violin, cello and baryton over the next ten years.

After the Prince had a new theatre built at Esterháza in 1768, Haydn spent a great deal of his time working with opera. He wrote an opera specially for the opening of the theatre, and other operas were written for special occasions like family weddings, or as special events for visiting dignitaries. Haydn not only wrote his own operas during these years, he also arranged and produced operas by other composers. The Empress Maria Theresa said she always went to Esterháza when she wanted to see a good opera. Prince Nikolaus added a marionette theatre to the facilities five years later, and Haydn wrote puppet operas for performance there as well. In addition to his opera work, Haydn wrote 15 masses, several oratorios and a number of cantatas, both religious and non-religious.

An opera at Esterháza. You can see the orchestra at the bottom, and the composer conducting from the keyboard.

The established composer

Haydn's reputation as a composer grew steadily. He had been publishing his compositions for some years, so even though he had been isolated at Esterháza, his music was very popular. When he was asked to do a concert series in London, England, he agreed to compose an opera, six symphonies and several other concert works, and to go to London to conduct these works.

Haydn very much enjoyed the rich cultural life in London. People made a great fuss over him, and he met everyone who mattered. When Haydn returned to Vienna, he was an international celebrity with a Doctor of Music degree from Oxford University. Haydn went back to London for another concert season two years later, which was again very successful. He became a favourite of the British royal family.

At the end of his life, Haydn was able to live in Vienna. He continued to compose and conduct, and publish new works. When his wife died in 1800, Haydn was too old to remarry. Living alone in his house in Vienna, he was much valued by the Viennese people. He was made an honorary citizen of Vienna, and received honours from royalty. Haydn was not strong in these later years. His final appearance as a conductor was in 1803, and he was carried in a sedan chair to attend his last concert in 1808. Haydn grew progressively weaker until he died in May of 1809. It was reported that the "whole art-loving world of Vienna" attended his memorial service.

Portrait of Haydn painted on his first visit to London

Haydn was very kind, and his musicians and his friends all called him "Papa." He said himself, "Anyone can see by the looks of me that I am a very good-natured sort of fellow."

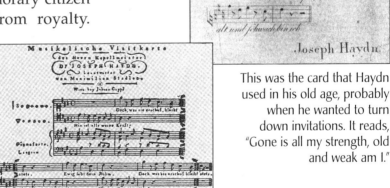

This was the card that Haydn used in his old age, probably when he wanted to turn down invitations. It reads, "Gone is all my strength, old and weak am I."

Haydn's visiting card

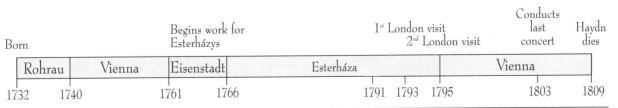

Born			Begins work for Esterházys			1ˢᵗ London visit 2ⁿᵈ London visit			Conducts last concert	Haydn dies
Rohrau	Vienna		Eisenstadt		Esterháza				Vienna	
1732	1740		1761	1766			1791	1793	1795	1803	1809

Symphonies

Haydn has been called "the father of the symphony" because he, more than any other composer, created the symphony in the Classical style. Mozart and Beethoven were building on his work when they developed their own symphonies.

He wrote 105 symphonies over the course of his career. The earliest show Haydn working out the general form of the symphony and developing it. Then he went through a period where he composed a series of very different symphonies. They were much more expressive, and were written in minor keys, which was unusual for the period. Scholars have called this time in Haydn's life his "Sturm und drang" (storm and stress) period, after a style of German literature that dealt with gloomy subjects such as despair, suicide and madness. After this period, Haydn's symphonies are less intense and have elements of his sense of humour worked into them.

Some of Haydn's most popular symphonies today are the *Paris* symphonies, which he composed for a series of concerts in Paris, and the *London* symphonies, the ones he wrote during his two trips to London. Many of these symphonies have nicknames. *La reine*, no. 85, was so called because it was a favourite of Marie Antoinette, the Queen of France. Among the London symphonies, *The Surprise*, no. 94, contains a great crash on all the instruments to wake up the sleepers in the audience, *The Military*, no. 100, is full of the sounds of battle, *The Clock*, no.101, has ticking sounds in the slow movement, and *The Miracle*, no. 96, got its name because no one was hurt when a great chandelier fell to the ground during its first performance – everyone had crowded to the front of the platform to get a better view of the orchestra. (This event actually happened at the premiere performance of Symphony no. 102, but the nickname became attached to no. 96 for some reason.)

Authenticating 18th century compositions is very difficult because there were no copyright laws in existence. Publishers could bring out editions in any way they wanted, and might even put a fashionable composer's name on the work of another. Frequently we see contradictory numbers of compositions for composers in this period. The most up-to-date authority and the one used for this volume is *Baker's Biographical Dictionary*, 1992 edition.

Haydn's Compositions

105 symphonies
Symphonies to remember:
  Farewell Symphony, no. 45
  Paris Symphonies, nos. 82–87
  • *La reine*, no. 85
London Symphonies, nos. 93–104
  • *Surprise*, no. 94
  • *Miracle*, no. 96
  • *Military*, no. 100
  • *Clock*, no. 101
  • *London*, no. 104

Sinfonia concertante, no. 105

Chamber and keyboard music

Haydn wrote over 67 string quartets, 29 piano trios, and about 62 piano sonatas. In many ways, Haydn can also be called the "father of the string quartet." The string quartet was then seen as music for connoisseurs, and in them, Haydn was able to explore his ideas without having to worry about the music being too hard for the audience to understand. They are still popular today and are among the most frequently performed quartets in the literature. His piano sonatas are still part of the repertoire of every advanced piano student and many professional musicians include them in their concerts.

Haydn's Compositions

67 string quartets

29 piano trios

62 piano sonatas

The title page of a set of six sonatas that Haydn dedicated to Prince Nikolaus I. Notice how large the Prince's name is compared to Haydn's.

Haydn and his friends playing quartets. Haydn is on the right, turning the page. Haydn and Mozart became friends and they often played string quartets together.

Vocal music

Haydn's Compositions

24 operas (4 lost)
5 oratorios
15 masses

Works to remember:
Opera
• *Il mondo della luna*

Oratorios:
• *The Creation*
• *The Seasons*

Masses:
• *Mass in Time of War*
• *Nelson Mass*

Haydn wrote 24 operas of which four have been lost. Only one of them, *Il mondo della luna*, is performed regularly now, but they were very popular and influential in their day. He was a proponent of the new idea that the *opera seria* should be more natural. It is only in recent years that many of Haydn's operatic works have become available for study, and he is now seen as a very important link to Mozart in both his Italian and German-language operas.

In his later years, Haydn concentrated on choral music. He had written masses before, but hearing Handel's choral music in London inspired him to return to sacred choral works. He wrote six new masses in seven years. Two refer to the political situation at the time, when the French army under Napoleon was threatening all of Europe. These are the *Missa in tempore belli* (Mass in Time of War), and the *Nelson* Mass, celebrating British admiral Lord Nelson's victory over the French fleet.

Handel also inspired Haydn to write his two most famous oratorios. One was *The Creation*, which tells the story of how God created the world. It contains some of Haydn's most beautiful music, describing the creation of different animals, the rolling sea, the flowers in the meadows, as well as great dramatic choruses like the one illustrating God's bringing of light into the world. *The Seasons* was Haydn's last major work. It tells of the cycle of life in the countryside, in four distinct sections. Haydn said later that he should never have attempted the work, that it wore him out.

This picture of a special performance of *The Creation* to mark Haydn's 76th birthday was originally painted in miniature on a box lid. The box has unfortunately been lost. You can see Haydn sitting in the centre foreground.

Family

Wolfgang Amadeus Mozart was born in Salzburg, Austria on January 27, 1756. His father, Leopold, was a violinist and composer at the court of the Archbishop of Salzburg. Leopold and his wife had seven children altogether but, as was often the case in those days, only two lived past childhood. These were Wolfgang and his sister Maria Anna, nicknamed Nannerl, who was five years older.

Leopold Mozart,
Wolfgang's father

Anna Maria Pertl Mozart,
Wolfgang's mother

The house where Mozart was born

This is an illustration from Leopold Mozart's violin method book showing the correct way to hold the instrument.

A child prodigy

Nannerl began to study piano when she was seven, and showed real talent. Wolfgang was even more precocious, however. When he was four, he began to play some of her pieces, and when he was five, composed two short pieces himself. Mozart had perfect pitch and he could hear a note and identify it without having to pick it out on the keyboard. At the age of seven, he was able to sight read a second violin part perfectly, even though no one had ever taught him how to play the violin. Leopold Mozart decided that Wolfgang was a prodigy, a child with extraordinary talents for his years. He also decided that there was no reason that the family should not benefit from these talents, and he began exhibiting the two children at concerts and in performances for the nobility, who might be expected to reward the children in some significant way. During the children's concerts, Wolfgang would display his genius by improvising, sight-reading, and naming notes that were sounded. He also impressed audiences of the time by playing with a cloth over the keyboard.

As a child prodigy, Mozart was the object of a great deal of curiosity. At one point, he was examined by a scientist to prove that he was really a boy and not a midget. The real proof came when a cat wandered into the room and Wolfgang could not be persuaded to return to the piano. He also spent some time riding around the room on a stick, pretending it was a horse. By acting like a child, Mozart established that he was one.

This painting shows Leopold playing the violin while Nannerl sings and Wolfgang plays piano.

These are a few bars of a minuet composed by Mozart when he was six years old.

Mozart's first composition, which he wrote at the age of five

Travelling musicians: Vienna

When Wolfgang was six, the family went to Vienna, and the children spent over three months playing for various aristocratic patrons including the Empress Maria Theresa. The Empress sent Wolfgang and Nannerl each a set of elegant court clothes. Wolfgang amused everyone, and embarrassed his father, by proposing marriage to the Empress's daughter, Marie Antoinette, who later became Queen of France.

Born		Performs for the Empress
	Salzburg	Vienna
1756		1762

Mozart and his sister Nannerl in the outfits presented to them by the Empress Maria Theresa of Austria

Six-year-old Wolfgang plays for the royal family in Vienna.

Mozart bows after playing the piano for the Empress and her court.

Travelling musicians: Paris and London

In 1763, when Mozart was seven, his father decided that he should take his children to the largest and most important musical centres in Europe, Paris and London. They travelled in their own stagecoach, stopping at all the important musical places on the way. They spent five months in Paris and played for King Louis XV at his Palace of Versailles. While he was there, Mozart had his music published for the first time.

The family moved on to London, where they stayed more than a year. Mozart played at concerts and at the court of King George III, and composed his first symphonies. The family became friends with Johann Christian Bach, another of Johann Sebastian's musician sons. He and Mozart played together on the harpsichord, and Mozart studied his compositions. Then, when Wolfgang was ten years old, the family returned to Salzburg.

Johann Christian Bach

An advertisement for one of Wolfgang and Nannerl's recitals

To all Lovers of Sciences.

THE greatest Prodigy that Europe, or that even Human Nature has to boast of, is, without Contradiction, the little German Boy WOLFGANG MOZART; a Boy, Eight Years old, who has, and indeed very justly, raised the Admiration not only of the greatest Men, but also of the greatest Musicians in Europe. It is hard to say, whether his Execution upon the Harpsichord and his playing and singing at Sight, or his own Caprice, Fancy, and Compositions for all Instruments, are most astonishing. The Father of this Miracle, being obliged by Desire of several Ladies and Gentlemen to postpone, for a very short Time, his Departure from England, will give an Opportunity to hear this little Composer and his Sister, whose musical Knowledge wants not Apology. Performs every Day in the Week, from Twelve to Three o'Clock in the Great Room, at the Swan and Hoop, Cornhill. Admittance 2s. 6d. each Person.

The two Children will play also together with four Hands upon the same Harpsichord, and put upon it a Handkerchief, without seeing the Keys.

		Performs for the Empress	Begins touring at age 7		Back home
Born	Salzburg	Vienna	Paris	London	Salzburg
1756		1762	1763	1764	1765

Mozart playing the harpsichord at a tea party given by the Prince de Conti in Paris

Travelling musicians: Italy

When Mozart was 13, his father took him to Italy on the same kind of tour they had taken before, stopping and giving concerts wherever there was an audience who would pay to hear Mozart play.

Mozart and his father made three more trips to Italy over the next two years, and he used his time in Italy to study opera and begin composing operas of his own. He also made quite a lot of money with his performances, but he did not succeed in finding work at any of the royal courts.

In Rome, Mozart and his father went to the Sistine Chapel to hear Gregorio Allegri's *Miserere*, a piece composed for the choir there, and never performed anywhere else. Mozart wrote out the score of the work after hearing it once.

Mozart wearing the insignia of a Knight of the Order of the Golden Spur conferred on him in Rome by the Pope

Working for the Archbishop of Salzburg

Following his father's footsteps, Mozart was taken into the service of the Archbishop of Salzburg. Wolfgang was given a job as a concertmaster. Except for a short leave of absence to go to Paris when he was 21, Mozart spent the next four years in Salzburg, occupied with the routine duties of his job with the Archbishop.

In 1780, he received a commission to write an opera for a carnival in Munich. Called *Idomeneo*, it is considered Mozart's first great opera. Mozart went to Munich to finish writing the work, and stayed on afterwards, enjoying his success and his freedom. Soon, however, the Archbishop of Salzburg went to Vienna for the festivities honouring the new Emperor Joseph II, and he insisted that Mozart join his entourage.

In Vienna, Mozart was extremely unhappy with the Archbishop's treatment of him. Fresh from being a celebrity in Munich, he was back to being a servant. He had to eat in the kitchen and his status was lower than the valets, the servants who shaved the Archbishop and looked after his clothes. Worse yet, the Archbishop would not let him give concerts where he could earn money for himself. On one particular evening, the Archbishop would not release him to play at a concert the Emperor was attending, where he could have earned the equivalent of a half-year's salary. Finally Mozart and the Archbishop had a terrible argument. Mozart submitted a letter of resignation and was thrown out with a kick in the pants from the Archbishop's steward. Leopold Mozart was furious with his son, but Wolfgang insisted that his honour prevented him from continuing to work in such degrading circumstances.

Archbishop Colloredo
of Salzburg

The 21-year-old Mozart in Paris

Title page from the score of *Idomeneo*

Love and marriage

When Mozart left the service of the Archbishop, he had to leave his residence as well, and he found a place to live in the home of some old friends, the Webers. He became interested in their daughter, Constanze, and six months later, he wrote his father for permission to marry her.

Leopold Mozart gave permission for his son to marry, although he never approved of his daughter-in-law and her family. Wolfgang was very fond of Constanze, though, and the letters he wrote to her whenever they were apart show that they had a very affectionate relationship. They had six children altogether, but only two lived, Carl Thomas, born in 1784 and Franz Xaver, in 1790.

Constanze Weber

The Mozarts always seem to have been short of money, and we have grown used to hearing that they lived in poverty. His income certainly fluctuated, but he was in fact very well paid for his work. It seems quite likely that the couple had an expensive lifestyle and spent everything he earned as soon as they got it. They liked to entertain, dress well, go to parties and balls, and keep a carriage, all of which costs money. According to his sister, Nannerl, Mozart was incapable of managing his finances and Constanze was unable to help him.

Mozart's two children,
Carl and Franz

A freelance musician

The story is told that after Emperor Joseph II saw *The Abduction from the Seraglio* he said, "Too many notes, my dear Mozart." Mozart is reported to have replied, "Exactly the necessary number, your majesty."

Mozart began his freelance career by taking a few students, composing some smaller works and playing concerts at homes of the aristocracy. He also was asked to work on a new opera, this one based on a Turkish story. Austria was at war with Turkey, and things to do with Turkey were all the rage. It was a Singspiel, a comic opera written in German with some spoken dialogue, and it was called *Die Entführung aus dem Serrail*, or *The Abduction from the Seraglio*. It was well received, and Gluck, who was the most important opera composer in Vienna at the time, asked for an extra performance.

Born		Begins touring at age 7		Working for the Archbishop			Freelance musician
Salzburg		Vienna - Paris - London	Salzburg - Italy	Salzburg	Paris	Salzburg	Vienna
1756		1763	1769	1775	1778	1779	1781

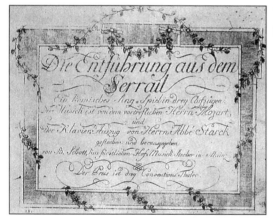

Title page from *The Abduction from the Seraglio*

A scene from
The Abduction from the Seraglio

More operas

Mozart's next major project was the comic opera, *The Marriage of Figaro*. This was Mozart's first collaboration with Lorenzo da Ponte, who wrote the opera's text, called the libretto. It was the first of three such collaborations. *Figaro* was moderately well received in Vienna and an enormous success in Prague, the capital of Bohemia. Here Mozart was commissioned to write another opera, and he and Da Ponte began work on *Don Giovanni*. Again, the opera was very popular in Prague but less so in Vienna. Mozart began work on his third opera with Da Ponte, *Così fan tutte* (Women are like that), but the Emperor unfortunately died soon after it opened, and all the theatres were closed for a mourning period.

Mozart began work on another opera with a different collaborator, his friend Emanuel Schikaneder, who was an actor-manager in his own theatre. *Die Zauberflöte*, or *The Magic Flute*, was another Singspiel. At the same time as Mozart was working on *The Magic Flute*, he was asked to write another opera for the coronation of the new King of Bohemia. It was an opera seria called *La Clemenza de Tito* (The Clemency of Titus) about a Roman emperor who pardons his enemies. He wrote the opera very quickly — its first performance was only two weeks after he began work on it.

Lorenzo da Ponte, the witty ex-priest who wrote the librettos for three of Mozart's operas

An announcement of the first performance of *The Marriage of Figaro*

A successful composer

You will usually see the letter K plus a number written after the names of Mozart's compositions, such as the Piano Concertos No. 20, K. 466, and No. 21, K. 467. This is because a man named Köchel (pronounced kershel) made an index of all Mozart's compositions in the order in which he wrote them, and gave every piece a number.

Over the next few years, Mozart's career consisted of teaching, performing and publishing his compositions. The many commissions he received are an indication of his success. In addition to his operas, Mozart composed works in all the other kinds of music written during the Classical period — chamber music, keyboard music, orchestral and vocal music. He was undoubtedly the most versatile composer of his time, and perhaps of any time in the history of Western music.

When his father visited in 1785, Mozart appeared to be doing very well indeed. Mozart counted Haydn as a friend, and had dedicated six string quartets to him. Haydn told Leopold Mozart, "Before God and as an honest man, I tell you that your son is the greatest composer known to me in person or in name."

Title page of the six string quartets dedicated to Haydn

The Requiem and Mozart's death

In 1791, Mozart was commissioned by a stranger to write a requiem, or mass for the dead. The stranger insisted on complete secrecy, and only later was he revealed to be an Austrian count whose wife had recently died and who wanted to claim that he had written the requiem himself. Mozart began to compose the requiem even though he was sick. As he worked, his health gradually grew worse, and he apparently became obsessed with the idea that he was writing his own funeral mass.

Mozart was not able to finish the *Requiem* in time. He took to his bed with a fever at the end of November and on December 5, 1791, at the age of 35, he died. Modern doctors have analysed his symptoms as they were recorded at the time, and have diagnosed his illness as rheumatic fever.

This unfinished portrait of Mozart was done by his brother-in-law, Josef Lange.

After a small funeral, Mozart was buried in a communal grave in a churchyard outside Vienna with no grave marker. A great deal has been said about Mozart having been too poor for a decent funeral, but mass graves, no mourners and no headstone were customary in Austria at the time. There were many memorial concerts and benefit concerts for Constanze, and the obituaries written about him recognized what a great composer he had been.

Constanze Mozart later remarried, and she and her second husband were responsible for preserving much of Mozart's work. She made sure that none of his compositions were published unless they were authentically his, and her husband wrote a very detailed biography of the composer.

Statue of Mozart in Salzburg

	Born	Begins touring at age 7			Working for the archbishop		Freelance musician	Marriage		Collaboration with Da Ponte	Death
	Salzburg	Vienna - Paris - London	Salzburg - Italy	Salzburg		Paris	Salzburg	Vienna			
	1756	1763	1769	1775		1778	1779	1781	1782	1785	1791

Operas

Mozart's opera music is his greatest achievement. He was a master of all the kinds of opera that were common in his day: *opera seria*, or serious Italian opera, *opera buffa*, or the lighter, comic Italian opera, and *Singspiel*, comic opera written in German with spoken dialogue. He used his music to express character and humanity better than any other composer before him and, some would say, since. The people in his operas really come to life as human beings. He accomplished this not just with the vocal music but the orchestral accompaniment as well.

Mozart's Compositions

16 operas

Operas to remember
* *Idomeneo*
* *The Abduction from the Seraglio*
* *The Marriage of Figaro*
* *Don Giovanni*
* *Così fan tutti*
* *The Magic Flute*

Title page from the score of *The Marriage of Figaro*

The Marriage of Figaro is based on a French play about a clever valet, Figaro, who wants to marry a maid named Susanna, but has to outwit the Count, their master, who wants Susanna for himself. The music sung by the Count and his wife has a very different tone from that sung by his servant Figaro and the maid Susanna, illustrating the difference in their social class. It shows the Count's anger and jealousy when he thinks about Figaro getting Susanna when he will not, and Figaro's distrust for women when he thinks Susanna has betrayed him. The music sung by Cherubino, the teen-age page boy, brings out all his youth and desire.

Don Giovanni is a retelling of the story of Don Juan, the infamous seducer of women, who ends up in Hell when he refuses to make amends for his misdeeds. The story has serious aspects that make it a less obvious choice for a comic opera. Some authorities have suggested that it could be called "heroicomic." Audiences have always responded to the excitement of the supernatural in the scene where the statue of a man Giovanni has murdered comes to life and drags him down to Hell for what Giovanni did to his daughter.

Title page from the score of *Don Giovanni*

Operas

*T*he *Magic Flute* tells the story of Prince Tamino's rescue of Pamina, the daughter of the Queen of the Night. It seems almost like a fairy tale, with characters like Prince Tamino and Princess Pamina, Sarastro the wicked magician, Papageno the comic bird-catcher, and Pamina's mother, the Queen of the Night. However, Mozart wove serious elements into the opera, as well as ritual aspects of Freemasonry that clearly relate to the philosophical ideals of the Enlightenment. The Masonic symbols have caused much controversy over the years— Mozart was accused of betraying the organization's secrets. Some historians have suggested, however, that he was using them to illustrate his idea of the perfect society. *Figaro, Don Giovanni* and *The Magic Flute* are Mozart's most popular operas with modern audiences.

Freemasonry was a secret organization that existed all over Europe and England. The members, many of whom were rich and powerful men, believed in the ideals of the Enlightenment, like equality and the brotherhood of Man.

Sacred Compositions

16 masses

Works to remember
* *Mass in C minor*
* *Requiem* (unfinished)

Sacred vocal music

In addition to his operatic vocal writing, Mozart wrote a great deal of sacred music. Best known are the *Mass in C minor* and the *Requiem*, but he wrote 13 other masses and a number of other shorter sacred works

Title page from the libretto of *The Magic Flute*

Papageno the bird-catcher from *The Magic Flute*

Orchestral works

Mozart's Compositions

Symphonies: 41

Concertos:
5 violin
27 piano
other instruments

Divertimentos, serenades, marches and dances

Works to remember:
Symphonies:
- *Haffner*, no. 35, K.385
- *Linz*, no. 36, K. 425
- *Prague*, no. 38, K.543
- *Jupiter*, no. 41, K.551

Serenades
- *Eine kleine Nachtmusik*

Mozart wrote over 40 symphonies. Most important are the six that he wrote in the last ten years of his life, ending with the "Jupiter", No. 41 in C major, K. 551. They are noted for the richness of their orchestration and the emotion that they are able to communicate.

As a virtuoso pianist, Mozart naturally wrote concertos for piano and orchestra—there are more than 20 of them. Keyboard concertos were very popular and Mozart developed the form to perfection. Mozart also wrote many concertos for violin, as well as other less commonly highlighted instruments such as the French horn and the clarinet.

There are also many miscellaneous orchestral works written for social occasions, such as the divertimenti and the serenades. The Serenades in E flat major, K. 375, and C minor, K. 388, for instance, are written for groups of wind instruments. The most famous of Mozart's party music is undoubtedly the Serenade in G, K. 525, known as "Eine kleine Nachtmusik (A Little Night Music)."

Mozart's first Horn Concerto

Chamber and keyboard music

Mozart's string quartets are among the finest ever written. He wrote 30, among them the six that he dedicated to Joseph Haydn, his "most celebrated and very dear friend". He also wrote two string quintets, for two violins, two violas and cello, and the Quintet for Clarinet, K. 581. Mozart's violin sonatas are very well known and frequently performed.

In addition to the keyboard concertos discussed previously, Mozart composed a large number of works for piano alone, or for another solo instrument, as well as piano duets with string or wind instruments. His Quintet for piano and wind, K.452, is particularly interesting, in view of the difficulty of writing for the wind instruments of the time, which had trouble sustaining long notes. He wrote 40 piano sonatas, including the A minor Sonata, K. 330, which was composed in Paris when his mother died. The Fantasia in C minor, K. 475, and the Fantasia in D minor, K. 397, are familiar works to piano students.

Mozart's Compositions

Chamber music:
 30 string quartets
 2 string quintets
 1 clarinet quintet
 6 piano trios
 47 violin sonatas

Keyboard music
 40 piano sonatas, 4 lost
 2 piano quartets
 Piano quintet with winds

Works to remember:
 • *Haydn* quartets
 • *Fantasia* in C minor, K. 475
 • *Rondo in A minor*, K. 511

The Mozart family playing chamber music.

Mozart and his sister are at the piano, and his father is shown with his violin. Mozart's mother, who died two years before this picture was painted, is shown in the portrait on the wall.

Family background and musical education

Ludwig van Beethoven was born in 1770 in Bonn, part of what is now called Germany. His grandfather was a singer and kapellmeister, or music director, to the Archbishop-Elector of Cologne, one of the many German states. His father too was a singer at the same court, and taught singing as well as piano and violin. When Ludwig showed some musical promise, he was given piano and violin lessons, and gave his first public performance at the age of seven, playing some keyboard concertos. He was not an obvious prodigy like Mozart, and stories are told that his father kept him at the keyboard for hours in tears.

Beethoven went to the local elementary school and never had more than three years of formal education. All his life he had trouble with spelling and ordinary arithmetic. His musical education included piano, organ, violin and music theory. By the time Ludwig was $11\frac{1}{2}$, he was occasionally asked to be the court organist. He also played the harpsichord in the court orchestra and published his first composition, three piano sonatas, at the age of 12.

The house where Beethoven was born

Beethoven began to give lessons to help support his family when he was 14 years old. His mother had tuberculosis and his father, whose talents were in decline, began to drink heavily. Two years later, Ludwig was given the opportunity to go to Vienna where he had some lessons from Mozart, but he had to return home after only two weeks because his mother became very ill. She died shortly afterwards, and his father became even more difficult as time wore on. Beethoven shouldered most of the responsibility for his two brothers.

Johann van Beethoven, Ludwig's father

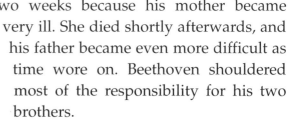

An engraving of Beethoven's mother, Maria Magdalena Keverich

Moving to Vienna

By the time Beethoven was 20, he began to attract quite a bit of attention in his hometown of Bonn. A group of influential people encouraged Beethoven, gave him money, and made it possible for him to go to Vienna to study with Haydn.

In 1792, at the age of 22, Beethoven arrived in Vienna. Shortly thereafter he began his lessons with Haydn, but they were not a great success. Beethoven felt he wasn't learning enough. When Haydn went to London, Beethoven turned to Johann Albrechtsberger, the best known counterpoint teacher in Vienna, and also Antonio Salieri, Mozart's old rival, who helped him learn to put Italian words to music.

Beethoven began quickly to make his mark on Vienna as a pianist and composer. His connections in Bonn led to introductions into Viennese society. Prince Lichnowsky, who had also befriended Mozart, was his first patron. Beethoven performed with enormous success at musical salons and charity concerts. His first concert tour was very successful and by the time he was 27 years old, he was virtually unrivalled as a concert pianist in Vienna.

It is interesting that Beethoven seems to have been accepted so readily by the elite of Vienna. He was not a handsome man, rather short, with a pock-marked face, and he did not seem to care about how he looked. Moreover, his manners were not polished. He refused to bow and scrape to the nobility and conform to their standards of behaviour. In later life he seemed to act as if he thought his music entitled him to behave as though he were royalty.

The young Beethoven

This drawing is a cartoon of Beethoven on one of his famous long solitary walks around Vienna. Dressed in black and looking at his feet, he is apparently lost in thought, and ignoring his fellow composer Schubert, who is shown bowing to him in the foreground.

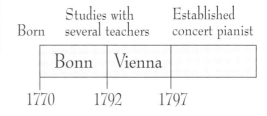

Born	Studies with several teachers	Established concert pianist
	Bonn	Vienna	
1770	1792	1797

Becoming established as a composer

In 1800, Beethoven's First Symphony was performed. It was a slight departure from the Classical model but in spite of its newness was quite well received. In April of 1803, the First Symphony was performed again, along with the Second Symphony and his new oratorio, *The Mount of Olives*, all at the same concert. What a long evening that must have been!

Here is the famous theme from the last movement of the *Eroica*. Beethoven used it in three other compositions, including the *Eroica* Variations

During these years, Beethoven was busy composing piano sonatas and string quartets as well. He also began work on a mammoth new symphony, his third. Much longer than any symphony previously written, it was originally dedicated to Napoleon Bonaparte, because Beethoven greatly admired the man he regarded as a hero risen from the people to save his country. However, when Napoleon had the audacity to crown himself emperor, Beethoven was outraged. For him, emperors were the same as tyrants. He tore the title page of the symphony in two and removed the dedication. It has been known as the "Eroica" ever since — still dedicated to the heroic spirit, but no longer to Napoleon.

Beethoven's work continued to be popular with the Viennese public, and in 1809 this success brought him financial security. Three of his aristocratic friends, Prince Lobkowitz, Prince Kinsky and the Archduke Rudolph, who was the Emperor's brother, signed a contract that provided Beethoven with a guaranteed annual income for the rest of his life.

Beethoven's patrons:
Prince Lobkowitz
Prince Ferdinand Kinsky
Archduke Rudolph von Hapsburg

	Born	Studies with several teachers	Established concert pianist	Established composer	Financial security
		Bonn	Vienna		
	1770	1792	1797	1800	1809

Becoming established as a composer

The heroic outlook of the Third Symphony continued into Beethoven's only opera. *Fidelio* tells of a brave woman's fight to rescue her husband from prison, and the heroine sums up Beethoven's notion of the ideal woman. He found the opera very difficult to compose, and rewrote the overture four times. *Fidelio* had its first performance just after Napoleon's troops had marched into Vienna and it closed after only three nights. It was not a time for going to the theatre. He reworked the opera, cutting the three acts down to two, but it still met with only limited success. Finally, in 1814, a revised version was produced and became very popular.

Beethoven carried on working at a great pace, and over the next three years he produced three more symphonies, various concertos, string quartets and the Mass in C, which was written for Prince Nikolaus Esterházy, Haydn's old employer.

Beethoven gave another marathon concert during this period. It was four hours long, and almost all the music was new. His Symphonies No. 5 and 6 were both played, along with his Fourth Piano Concerto, and parts of the Mass in C, with a Choral Fantasy for the finale. Beethoven quarrelled with the orchestra, the soprano quit, and the theatre was freezing cold. The concert was not a success.

Beethoven in 1804 or 1805

Inside the Theater-am-der-Wien where *Fidelio* was first performed

Problems and crises

Before he was even 30 years old, Beethoven realized that he was losing his hearing. Becoming deaf was a catastrophe — it meant his career as concert pianist would be effectively over. Even more disastrous was the effect on Beethoven's social life. He began to withdraw from people, because he could not bear to admit to them he was deaf, becoming more and more isolated, more and more depressed. After spending the summer of 1802 in a small village called Heiligenstadt, he set down his misery in a letter to his two brothers. The letter, found in his papers after his death, and called the "Heiligenstadt Testament," was never sent. It told of his hopelessness and despair, and admitted that he had thought of but rejected the idea of suicide. Perhaps writing it all down helped Beethoven conquer his depression, because after this he threw himself back into his work as if determined to triumph no matter what.

Beethoven's relationships with his brothers were often troubled. He disliked both his sisters-in-law, and fought often with his brothers. In 1815, his brother Caspar Carl became very ill and died. Beethoven got into a nasty court battle with his sister-in-law over who would be the legal guardian of his nine-year-old nephew, Karl. After four years, Beethoven finally won. But Karl was a difficult child, and his guardianship was not an easy one. After Karl tried to commit suicide at the age of 20, friends said that Beethoven turned into an old man overnight. Beethoven's musical output during the years in which he was consumed by the struggle for his nephew was rather slim.

"Such experiences have brought me close to despair, and I came near to ending my own life–only my art held me back, as it seemed to me impossible to leave this world until I have produced everything I feel it has been granted to me to achieve." From the Heiligenstadt Testament

Karl
Beethoven

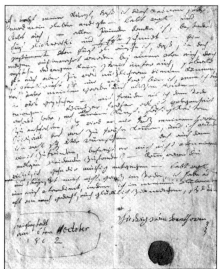

The last page of the Heiligenstadt Testament

A collection of
Beethoven's ear trumpets

Romantic involvements

Beethoven had a history of passionate attractions to unattainable women, who were either already married or were so far above him in social class that they would never have thought of marrying him. Even though Beethoven considered himself any man's equal, it was not so long since composers were looked upon as servants, no more valued than the cook.

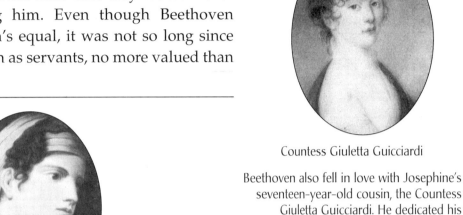

Countess Giuletta Guicciardi

Beethoven also fell in love with Josephine's seventeen-year-old cousin, the Countess Giuletta Guicciardi. He dedicated his famous *Moonlight* Sonata to her.

Josephine von Brunsvik   Therese von Brunsvik

In 1799, the Countesses Therese and Josephine von Brunsvik came to Vienna to take lessons from Beethoven and he became very attached to them, particularly to Josephine. However, she married a count who was 30 years her senior. When she was widowed, Beethoven courted her in earnest. She was never willing to marry him, though.

Für Elise, written for Therese Malfatti

Antonie Brentano and her two children

In the summer of 1812, Beethoven wrote a passionate love letter to an unknown woman he addressed only as "Immortal Beloved." It was found in his papers after his death, and the identity of this mystery woman has been long debated. The most likely candidate seems to be Antonie Brentano, a married aristocratic lady from Vienna. Beethoven had become friends with her and her family two years previously, and she admired him greatly. She never left her husband, however, and never saw Beethoven again after the summer of 1812. He remained a bachelor all his days.

Therese Malfatti

Then Beethoven formed an attachment for Therese Malfatti, his doctor's daughter. By this time he was 40 years old and she was only 18, and his proposal was turned down. *Für Elise*, familiar to generations of young pianists, was written for her.

The last decade

Beethoven's funeral procession

Even in the later years of his career, Beethoven continued to work hard. When his friend the Archduke Rudolph was made an archbishop in 1819, he began work on a high mass to be performed during the ceremonies. This became known as the *Missa solemnis*, Beethoven's most important piece of sacred music. He did not manage to finish it in time for the Archbishop's installation, and it was never performed in Vienna in his lifetime.

During this period, he completed two piano sonatas and the mass, and began work on his last and greatest symphony, the Ninth, which was to have a chorale finale, a setting of the *Ode to Joy* by the German poet Schiller. It took him nearly a year to write.

Beethoven in 1823. It may not be an accurate portrait, because it looks so different from the other pictures we have of him, but it certainly suggests the stubbornness and determination that were part of his character.

In 1824, he was begged to give another concert in Vienna, and some parts of the *Missa solemnis* and the whole Ninth Symphony were performed. The concert was a huge success. Beethoven did not conduct, but he stood on the stage directing the performance. When the audience broke out into wild cheers, Beethoven, turning pages in the score, did not hear a thing. One of the soloists pulled on his sleeve and pointed, whereupon he turned and took his bow.

Beethoven spent his remaining years working on string quartets. At the end of 1826 he returned ill from a stay in the country, suffering from swollen feet. The doctors diagnosed liver disease, but there was little they could do for him. He died on March 26, 1827. His funeral was a major event for the Viennese people. Ten thousand lined the streets to catch a last glimpse as the funeral procession passed.

Born	Studies with several teachers	Established concert pianist	Established composer	Financial security	Personal difficulties, output diminishes	Return to productivity	Complete deafness	Illness and death
	Bonn	Vienna						
1770	1792	1797	1800	1809	1813-1816	1817	1818	1827

A transitional composer

Beethoven is firmly rooted in the Classical style, and he believed in its principles. But he also was affected by the changes that came with and after the French Revolution. It was a time of heroes and great ideas, and we can see Beethoven's response to them in the evolution of his compositional style. His music shows excitement, struggle and tension very different from the elegance of Haydn and Mozart.

His work has traditionally been divided into three periods. In the first he learned to use the elements of music that had been handed down to him by Haydn and Mozart. In the second period, often called his "heroic" period, he intensified these elements to produce another kind of music, full of power and emotion. At the end of his life, he composed works that explored brand new ideas and opened up possibilities for later musicians to build on. He was an innovator who brought change in both style and form to the musical traditions that had come before him.

Beethoven is probably the most famous composer in the Western world. Even people who know nothing about classical music have heard of him. In our time, his music has spread beyond the concert hall to popular culture in movie soundtracks, advertising jingles and pop renderings of his melodies.

Ludwig van Beethoven

Sketches of Beethoven by Johann Peter

Symphonies

Beethoven's compositions

Nine symphonies

Works to remember:
- Symphony no. 3, *Eroica*
- Symphony no. 5 (with its famous four note motif)
- Symphony no. 6, *Pastoral*
- Symphony no. 9 (with the choral "Ode to Joy")

The theme from the first movement of the Symphony no. 5 in C minor, op. 67

The theme of the *Ode to Joy*

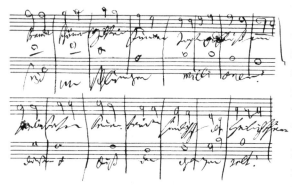

Beethoven wrote nine symphonies. The first two date from his early "Classical" period. It was not until the Third Symphony, the *Eroica*, that he showed his mature style: it had dramatic momentum with lots of contrast, and a powerful climax in the finale. Beethoven's Fifth is one of his most easily recognized — the four notes in the opening motif, three shorts and a long, are famous around the world. They were said to represent "fate knocking at the door." By the end of the symphony, the motif — which appears in all four movements — has changed from threat to jubilation.

The Sixth Symphony, the *Pastoral*, expresses Beethoven's ideas about the natural world, much more melodic and peaceful than the fifth. However, one of his strengths is the way he is able to include tender passages even in the most dramatic of his works. Perhaps his most enduringly popular work is the Ninth or *Choral* Symphony. In the last movement, a chorus and soloists join the orchestra and sing the words to the *Ode to Joy*, a poem by the great German poet Friederich von Schiller. In the Ninth, Beethoven expresses his feelings about the brotherhood of man, and the music has been inspirational to people all over the world.

Beethoven was the first composer to thoroughly link all the sections of his works, instead of writing entirely self-contained movements. His symphonies exerted such a strong influence that later composers were intimidated by them. Brahms waited until he was 40 to write his first symphony and Wagner stated that Beethoven had said all there was to say in symphony form. The nine symphonies are the basis of the repertoire of every modern orchestra in the Western world, and the ultimate test for a conductor.

Beethoven's sketch for the finale of the Ninth Symphony

Other orchestral works

In addition to his symphonies, Beethoven wrote a number of concertos, five for piano, one for violin and a triple concerto for piano, violin and cello. They were on a larger scale than the usual Classical concerto, and allowed the soloist to display a great deal of virtuosity within a symphonic type of structure. Beethoven wrote out the cadenzas for his later concertos, telling the soloist exactly what to play. He neither expected nor encouraged soloists to improvise, as was more common earlier in the period.

The piano sonatas

The piano sonatas that Beethoven wrote are very different from those of Mozart and Haydn. The earlier two composers generally adapted harpsichord technique to the new instrument, and the speed and dexterity needed to be a fine harpsichord player are hallmarks of their sonatas. By the time Beethoven was writing his sonatas, however, the piano had developed different characteristics—more resonance, and the ability to have much more variation in sound volume, which Beethoven used to great dramatic effect. The sonatas he wrote for piano demanded a whole new technique.

Beethoven's 32 piano sonatas are some of the most important works in all piano literature. Together with Bach's *Well-Tempered Clavier*, they have been called the pianist's Bible—Bach's work being the Old Testament and Beethoven's the New. The best known are the *Pathétique*, the *Moonlight*, the *Appassionata* and the *Waldstein*.

Beethoven's compositions

Five piano concertos
One violin concerto
One triple concerto for piano, violin and cello

32 piano sonatas
- *Pathétique* Sonata
- *Moonlight* Sonata
- *Appassionata* Sonata
- *Waldstein* Sonata

A silhouette of Beethoven at the piano

The piano that Beethoven used when he stayed at his brother's house in the country

Chamber music

Beethoven's compositions

17 string quartets
Other chamber music

Works to remember:
- *Razumovsky* quartets

One opera
Sacred choral works

Works to remember:
- *Fidelio*
- *Leonore* Overture
- *Missa solemnis*

Fidelio was not particularly well received at first. One reviewer wrote, "...never was anything as incoherent, shrill, chaotic, and ear-splitting produced in music."

Beethoven wrote string quartets throughout his life, 17 all told. The earlier ones are classical in style, but some of the quartets he wrote later are almost as long as symphonies. The well-known *Razumovsky* Quartets, dedicated to the Russian ambassador to Vienna, are based on Russian folk melodies. The five quartets he wrote at the end of his life are more abstract, more inward-looking, and his major achievement in writing for string quartet. Beethoven composed other chamber music as well—violin and cello sonatas, piano trios and quartets, and chamber music for wind instruments.

Vocal music

Fidelio, Beethoven's only opera, sits firmly in his heroic mode, telling of freedom and justice, and triumph over adversity. It also describes his ideal woman, brave, loyal and full of lofty ideals. The opera is not often performed today, but there are three versions of the *Leonore* overture that Beethoven wrote for different productions of the opera, and *Leonore* Nos. 2 and 3 are heard quite often at symphony concerts.

Beethoven's other major vocal work is his great mass, the *Missa solemnis*. The work is complex and challenging, blending Beethoven's intensely emotional response to his God with the traditional form of the Roman Catholic service. The way the composer integrated the soloists, choir and orchestra broke new ground.

Beethoven working on the *Missa solemnis*

This is the theatre where parts of the *Missa solemnis* was first performed

Printed in December 1998
Centre franco-ontarien de ressources pédagogiques